SINGER

SEWING REFERENCE LIBRARY

Embellished
Quilted Proj

COWLES
Creative Publishing

*A Division of Cowles Enthusiast Media, Inc.
Minnetonka, Minnesota, USA*

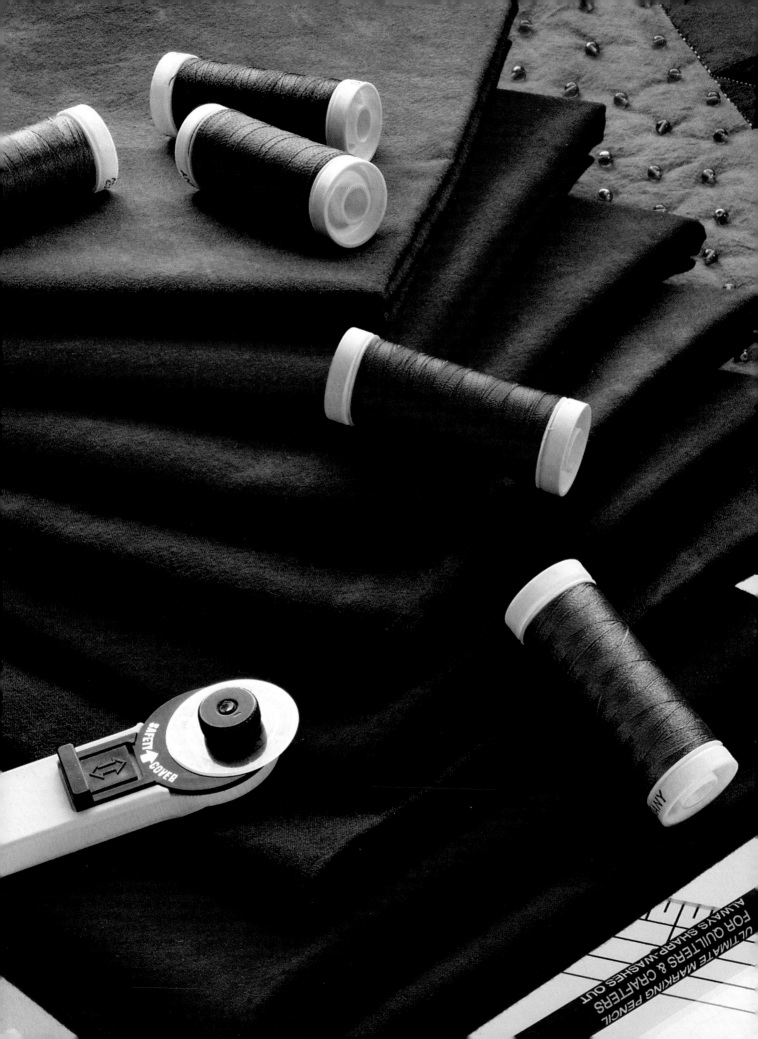

SINGER

SEWING REFERENCE LIBRARY®

Embellished Quilted Projects

Contents

Introduction **6**

Copyright © 1996
Cowles Creative Publishing, Inc.
Formerly Cy DeCosse Incorporated
5900 Green Oak Drive
Minnetonka, Minnesota 55343
1-800-328-3895
All rights reserved
Printed in U.S.A.

Also available from the publisher:
*Sewing Essentials, Sewing for the Home,
Clothing Care & Repair, Sewing for Style,
Sewing Specialty Fabrics, Sewing Activewear,
The Perfect Fit, Timesaving Sewing, More
Sewing for the Home, Tailoring, Sewing
for Children, Sewing with an Overlock,
101 Sewing Secrets, Sewing Pants That
Fit, Quilting by Machine, Decorative
Machine Stitching, Creative Sewing Ideas,
Sewing Lingerie, Sewing Projects for the
Home, Sewing with Knits, More Creative
Sewing Ideas, Quilt Projects by Machine,*
*Creating Fashion Accessories, Quick &
Easy Sewing Projects, Sewing for Special
Occasions, Sewing for the Holidays, Quick
& Easy Decorating Projects, Quilted
Projects & Garments*

Library of Congress
Cataloging-in-Publication Data

Embellished quilted projects.

p. cm. — (Singer sewing reference
library)
Includes index.
ISBN 0-86573-309-0
ISBN 0-86573-310-4 (pbk.)
1. Patchwork. 2. Machine quilting.
3. Fancy work. 4. Quilted goods.
I. Cy DeCosse Incorporated.
II. Series.
TT835.E484 1996
746.46 — dc20   96-32855

COWLES
Creative Publishing
A Division of Cowles Enthusiast Media, Inc.

President/COO: Nino Tarantino
Executive V. P./Editor-in-Chief:
  William B. Jones

EMBELLISHED QUILTED PROJECTS
Created by: The Editors of Cowles
Creative Publishing, in cooperation
with the Sewing Education
Department, Singer Sewing
Company. Singer is a trademark of
The Singer Company Limited and
is used under license.

Group Executive Editor: Zoe A. Graul
Editorial Manager: Dawn M. Anderson
Managing Editor: Elaine Johnson
Associate Creative Director: Lisa Rosenthal
Art Director: Linda Schloegel
Writers: Dawn M. Anderson, Ellen Boeke
Editor: Janice Cauley
Sample Production Manager: Carol Olson
Senior Technical Photo Stylist:
 Bridget Haugh
Technical Photo Stylists: Sue Jorgensen,
 Nancy Sundeen
Project & Prop Stylist: Joanne Wawra
Lead Samplemaker: Phyllis Galbraith
Sewing Staff: Arlene Dohrman, Bridget
 Haugh, Valerie Hill, Kristi Kuhnau,
 Virginia Mateen, Carol Pilot, Michelle
 Skudlarek, Sue Stein, Nancy Sundeen
V. P. Photography & Production: Jim Bindas
Studio Services Manager: Marcia Chambers
Creative Photo Coordinator:
 Cathleen Shannon

Lead Photographer: Rex Irmen
Photographer: Greg Wallace
Contributing Photographers: Billy Lindner,
 Steve Smith
Publishing Production Manager:
 Kim Gerber
Desktop Publishing Specialist:
 Laurie Kristensen
Production Staff: Tom Hoops,
 Mike Schauer, Kay Wethern
Shop Supervisor: Phil Juntti
Lead Carpenter: Troy Johnson
Consultants: Sharon Hultgren,
 Priscilla Miller, Barb Otto, Susan Stein,
 Donna Wilder
Contributors: American and Efird,
 Inc.; B. Blumenthal & Co., Inc.;
 Cherrywood Quilts & Fabrics;
 Coats & Clark Inc.; Concord House,
 Division of Concord Fabrics Inc.;
 Conso Products Company; Creative
 Beginnings; Dritz Corporation;

Dyno Merchandise Corporation;
EZ International; Fairfield Processing
Corporation; Hobbs Bonded Fiber;
HTC-Handler Textile Corporation;
Olfa® Products International;
Salem Rule; Source Marketing;
Speed Stitch, Inc.; Sulky of America;
YLI Corporation

COWLES
Enthusiast Media

President/COO: Philip L. Penny

Printed on American paper by:
Quebecor Printing
99 98 97 96 / 5 4 3 2 1

Introduction

Embellished Quilted Projects shows you how to create several embellished quilts for home decorating, as well as a variety of quilted garments and accessories with surface embellishments. Rotary cutting techniques and quick construction methods are used whenever possible. For projects that require templates, either the template pattern or the instructions for making the template are included with the project.

Silk ribbon embroidery enhances the floral motif on this Trip Around the World quilt (page 29).

The Quilt Projects for the Home section includes a variety of wall hangings. Choose from a Log Cabin quilt embellished with beaded tassels, a Lone Star wall hanging featuring yo-yo flowers and faced appliqués, or a wall hanging made of star blocks, accented with lace and ribbon trim. There is also a landscape sampler, featuring a wide variety of embellishment techniques, including raw-edge and blindstitched appliqué; lace, thread lace, and organza overlays; beads; and silk ribbon embroidery. Other projects for the home include a raw-edge Pinwheel design lap quilt, diamond-quilted and asymmetrically pieced pillows, and a Maple Leaf table runner.

In the Garments & More section, you'll find simple projects like a quilted sweatshirt, using the paper foundation piecing technique, and a toddler outfit embellished with a Noah's Ark appliqué design and animal buttons. More challenging projects include an organza and button vest and a bolero jacket that is motif-quilted and trimmed in silk ribbon embroidery. There is also an oversized market bag that features padded vegetable appliqués.

Stipple quilting and buttons embellish this sweatshirt (page 85).

The final section of the book is a reference section titled Quilt Basics. This section gives you the basic instructions for assembling a quilt. Learn everything you'll need to know about selecting fabrics, battings, cutting and piecing, basting the quilt layers together, quilting techniques, and applying the binding.

Quilt Projects for the Home

Log Cabin Stripe
Wall Hanging

Customize this simple wall hanging to go with any decorating style from country to contemporary, depending on the choice of fabrics. This quilt utilizes a combination of hand-dyed fabrics and a printed fabric. Beaded tassels embellish the centers of the Log Cabin blocks. And, for added interest, the wall hanging is quilted, using metallic thread. Light is reflected off the metallic thread, giving the quilt a shimmering look.

The hand-dyed fabrics used to produce the subtle color changes within the Log Cabin blocks are available in packets of eight coordinates at quilting shops and through mail-order suppliers.

The finished quilt measures about 45½" × 61½" (116 × 156.3 cm).

✂ Cutting Directions

Cut 1½" (3.8 cm) strips across the width of the fabric, for Fabrics A through I, for the Log Cabin blocks. Label the fabrics for the Log Cabin blocks as on page 12, step 1.

Cut three 5¾" × 36½" (14.5 × 91.8 cm) strips from printed fabric.

Cut six 1½" (3.8 cm) strips from the fabric for the inner border. Cut two strips to 36½" (91.8 cm) in length for the upper and lower inner borders. The side inner borders are cut on page 14, step 5. Cut six 4½" (11.5 cm) strips from the fabric for the outer border. Cut seven 2½" (6.5 cm) strips from the fabric for the binding.

YOU WILL NEED

½-yd. (0.5 m) bundle of eight hand-dyed fabrics in a light to dark gradation, for Log Cabin blocks; or ¼ yd. (0.25 m) each of Fabrics B, C, D, E, and F, and ⅜ yd. (0.35 m) each of Fabrics G, H, and I, and ⅛ yd. (0.15 m) Fabric A, for centers of Log Cabin blocks.

1⅛ yd. (1.05 m) printed fabric.

⅓ yd. (0.32 m) fabric, for inner border.

⅞ yd. (0.8 m) fabric, for outer border.

⅝ yd. (0.6 m) fabric, for binding.

2⅞ yd. (2.65 m) fabric, for backing.

Batting, about 50" × 64" (127 × 163 cm).

Metallic sewing thread, for quilting and thread tassels.

Embroidery thread, optional, for thread tassels.

Beads.

How to Sew Log Cabin Quilt Blocks

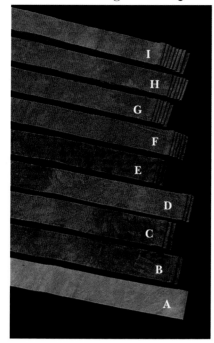

1) Cut fabrics for Log Cabin blocks as on page 11. Label strips from A to I as shown.

2) Stitch Strips A and B, right sides together, along one long edge. Press seam allowances away from Strip A. Cut across pieced strip at 1½" (3.8 cm) intervals to make sixteen units.

3) Stitch the pieced units to a second Strip B, using chainstitching as shown.

4) Trim Strip B even with edges of pieced units. Press seam allowances away from center squares.

5) Stitch the three-piece units to Strip C, using chainstitching; position units at 90° angle to most recent seam on side nearest center square. Trim Strip C even with edges of pieced units. Press seam allowances away from center squares.

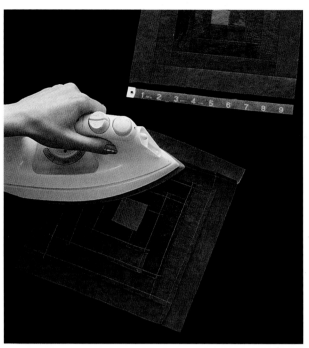

6) Stitch four-piece units to a second Strip C, using chainstitching; position units at 90° angle to the most recent seam on side nearest the center square. Trim Strip C even with edges of pieced units. Press seam allowances away from center squares.

7) Continue stitching two strips of Fabrics D, E, F, G, H, and I to pieced units in sequence. Press seam allowances away from center. The finished blocks measure 9½" (24.3 cm) square.

How to Sew a Log Cabin Stripe Wall Hanging

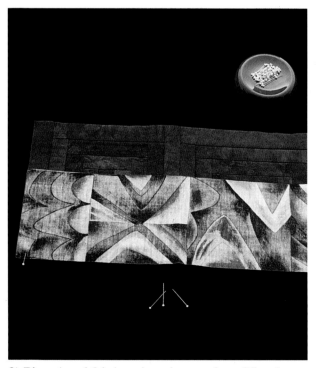

1) Stitch four Log Cabin blocks side by side, right sides together, to make a four-unit row. Finger-press seam allowances to one side. Repeat to make three more four-unit rows.

2) Pin printed fabric strip to lower edge of first Log Cabin row, at center and ends, right sides together; pin along the length, easing in any fullness. Stitch. Press seam allowances to one side.

(Continued on next page)

3) Continue stitching alternating rows of Log Cabin blocks and printed fabric strips together. Press the seam allowances to one side.

4) Pin the upper inner border strip to the upper edge of quilt top at center and ends, right sides together; pin along the length, easing in any fullness. Stitch. Repeat at lower edge. Press seam allowances toward inner borders.

5) Measure vertically through middle of quilt top, including inner border strips; cut two inner border strips for the sides equal to this length, piecing as necessary. Pin and stitch strips to sides of quilt top as in step 4.

6) Apply the outer border as on page 20, steps 6 to 8. Cut backing fabric 4" (10 cm) wider and longer than quilt top, piecing as necessary. Layer and baste the quilt as on page 117.

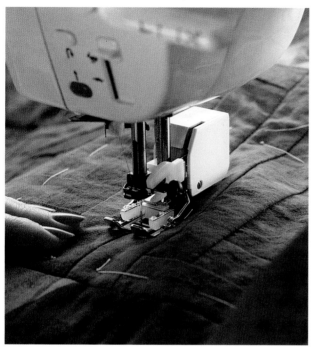

7) Quilt by stitching in the ditch (pages 118 and 120) between rows of printed fabric and rows of Log Cabin blocks. Stitch in the ditch between Log Cabin blocks. Stitch in the ditch on each side of inner border.

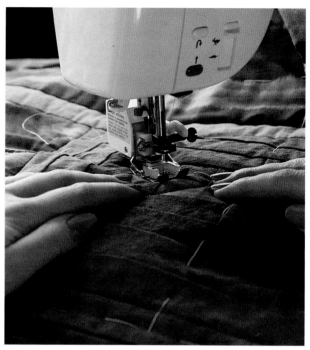

8) Stitch diagonally in both directions through Log Cabin blocks by making an X. Begin with a stitch length near 0 and gradually return to regular stitch length; end by reducing the stitch length to near 0. Quilt design motifs in printed fabric strips as desired (pages 118 and 120).

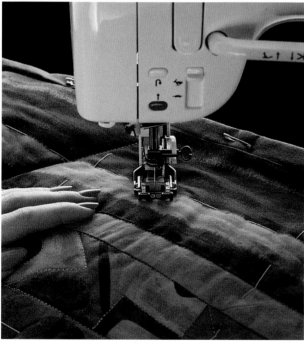

9) Quilt the outer border by stitching between inner border and binding in a zigzag pattern, using free-motion quilting and a walking foot (pages 118 and 120). Attach the fabric sleeve (page 124) and apply binding (pages 121 to 123).

10) Thread several strands of metallic or embroidery thread through needle. Stitch through center of each Log Cabin block, and knot by taking a backstitch; leave thread tails. Attach dangling beads among thread tails, using metallic or embroidery thread; string several beads together for a tassel effect, if desired.

Woven Stars Wall Hanging

This quilt pattern is made up of three modified Ohio Star quilt blocks of graduated sizes. The star block in the center of the quilt serves as the center square for the next larger star block. That resulting block, in turn, becomes the center square for the third and final star block.

Triangles for the quilt can be easily cut from strips of fabric, using Easy Angle™ cutting tools. Their use minimizes cutting time and effort. Instructions for traditional cutting methods are also given.

This quilted wall hanging is given an old-fashioned Victorian feel with lace, ribbon, braid trims, buttons, and charms. The lace, ribbons, and braid trims are pinned randomly from edge to edge across the quilt; then they are quilted onto the quilt top before the binding is applied.

The completed wall hanging measures approximately 39" (99 cm) square.

✂ Cutting Directions
(with the Easy Angle cutting tools)

Cut one 4½" (11.5 cm) square from the center fabric.

Cut one 2½" (6.5 cm) strip across the width of the background fabric and the star point fabric for the inner star. Cut eight triangles from each fabric strip as on page 18, steps 1 and 2. Cut four 2½" (6.5 cm) squares from the background fabric.

Cut one 4½" (11.5 cm) strip across the width of the background fabric and the star point fabric for the middle star. Cut eight triangles from each fabric strip as on page 18, step 3. Cut four 4½" (11.5 cm) squares from the background fabric.

Cut two 8½" (21.8 cm) strips across the width of the background fabric and one 8½" (21.8 cm) strip across the width of the star point fabric for the outer star. Cut eight triangles from each fabric as on page 18, step 3. Cut four 8½" (21.8 cm) squares from the background fabric.

Cut four 4" (10 cm) strips across the width of the border fabric.

Cut four 2" (5 cm) strips from the binding fabric.

✂ Cutting Directions
(without the Easy Angle cutting tools)

Cut one 4½" (11.5 cm) square from the center fabric.

Cut four 2⅞" (7.2 cm) squares each from the background fabric and the star point fabric for the inner star. Cut squares into triangles as on page 18. Cut four 2½" (6.5 cm) squares from the background fabric.

Cut four 4⅞" (12.2 cm) squares each from the background fabric and the star point fabric for the middle star. Cut squares into triangles as on page 18. Cut four 4½" (11.5 cm) squares from the background fabric.

Cut four 8⅞" (22.8 cm) squares each from the background fabric and the star point fabric for the outer star. Cut into triangles as on page 18. Cut four 8½" (21.8 cm) squares from the background fabric.

Cut four 4" (10 cm) strips across the width of the border fabric.

Cut four 2" (5 cm) strips from the binding fabric.

YOU WILL NEED

Fabric scrap, for center square.

⅛ yd. (0.15 m) fabric, for inner star background.

⅛ yd. (0.15 m) fabric, for inner star points.

¼ yd. (0.25 m) fabric, for middle star background.

¼ yd. (0.25 m) fabric, for middle star points.

⅝ yd. (0.6 m) fabric, for outer star background.

⅓ yd. (0.32 m) fabric, for outer star points.

½ yd. (0.5 m) fabric, for border.

1¼ yd. (1.15 m) fabric, for backing.

Batting, about 43" (109 cm) square.

¼ yd. (0.25 m) fabric, for binding.

7 to 10 yd. (6.4 to 9.15 m) lace or ribbon, of desired width.

Buttons or charms, for embellishing.

Easy Angle cutting tool, optional.

Easy Angle II cutting tool, optional.

1) With Easy Angle™ cutting tools. Align Easy Angle cutting tool with 2½" (6.5 cm) fabric strip at the marking for 2½" (6.5 cm) right triangle; cut along diagonal edge of tool.

2) Flip tool over, keeping diagonal edge of tool along diagonal cut of fabric. Align cutting tool with edge of fabric strip at the marking for 2½" (6.5 cm) right triangle; cut along straight edge of tool. Continue to cut necessary number of triangles (page 16).

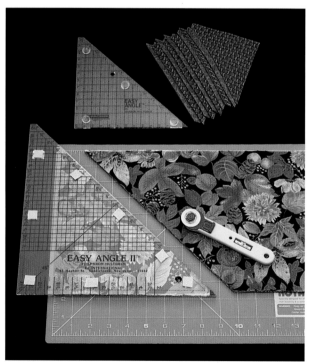

3) Repeat steps 1 and 2 for 4½" (11.5 cm) and 8½" (21.8 cm) strips, using Easy Angle II™ cutting tool for 8½" (21.8 cm) strips, and cutting the necessary number of triangles (page 16).

Without Easy Angle cutting tools. Layer four 2⅞" (7.2 cm) squares, matching raw edges; cut through squares diagonally. Repeat with remaining 2⅞" (7.2 cm) squares, the 4⅞" (12.2 cm) squares, and 8⅞" (22.8 cm) squares.

How to Sew a Woven Stars Wall Hanging

1) Stitch one triangle from inner star point fabric and one triangle from inner background fabric together, along the long edge, in ¼" (6 mm) seam. Continue piecing triangles until eight triangle-squares have been completed, using chainstitching as shown.

2) Repeat step 1 for middle and outer star fabric triangles. Clip units apart; press seam allowances toward darker fabric. Trim off points.

3) Arrange center fabric square, background fabric squares, and triangle-squares for inner star into quilt block design as shown.

4) Assemble block; finger-press seam allowances toward center square. Press block.

(Continued on next page)

5) Use inner star block as center square for middle star, and assemble middle star block as on page 19, steps 3 and 4. Repeat for the outer star block, using middle star block as center square, to complete the quilt top.

6) Measure horizontally through middle of quilt top, and cut two border strips to that length for upper and lower borders.

7) Pin upper border strip to upper edge of quilt top at center and ends, right sides together; pin along length, easing in any fullness. Stitch. Repeat at the lower edge. Press seam allowances toward borders.

8) Measure vertically through middle of quilt top, including border strips; cut two border strips for sides equal to this length. Pin and stitch strips to sides of quilt top as in step 7.

9) Cut backing fabric 4" (10 cm) wider and longer than quilt top, piecing as necessary. Layer and baste quilt top, batting, and backing as on page 117. Quilt, using stitch-in-the-ditch method (pages 118 and 120), in seamlines of stars and borders.

10) Pin strips of lace, ribbon, and braid trim in random diagonals across quilt top. Quilt along strips, stitching close to edges of wide trims and stitching down center of narrow trims.

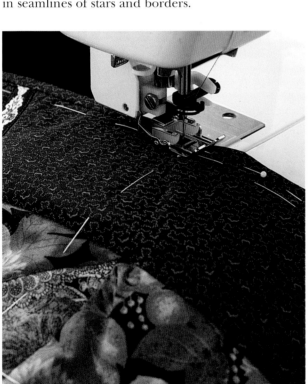

11) Attach fabric sleeve to wall hanging (page 124), and apply binding as on pages 121 to 123.

12) Embellish the quilt with buttons or charms as desired.

Zigzag Wall Hanging

Create the zigzag design in this wall hanging using a bundle of six hand-dyed fabrics. Choose a packet of fabrics that graduate in color value from light to dark, or select six different colors for a rainbow effect. For contrast, choose a printed fabric that coordinates with the hand-dyed packet to use along the upper and lower edges of the zigzag pattern.

The pieced portion of the quilt top inside the borders can be created either by using the templates on page 27 or by using a set of triangle quilting tools for cutting triangles within squares. The set of quilter's tools comes with a tool for cutting a wide triangle and a tool for cutting a narrow triangle. Stitching two narrow triangles to a wide triangle makes a triangles-within-a-square unit. The triangle pieces are stitched together in the order shown in the diagram on page 27 to produce the zigzag effect. The wall hanging is quilted with decorative thread and is embellished along the quilting lines with coordinating beads.

The finished quilt measures about 42" × 44" (107 × 112 cm).

✂ Cutting Directions

From each hand-dyed fabric, cut three 4½" (11.5 cm) strips; cut the strips to make nine wide triangles and eighteen narrow triangles, using the quilting tools or templates as shown below. From the printed fabric, cut three 4½" (11.5 cm) strips; cut the strips to make thirty-four wide triangles and four narrow triangles, using the quilting tools or templates as shown below. From the printed fabric, also cut one 6½" (16.3 cm) strip for the upper border. From the solid-colored fabric, cut three 4½" (11.5 cm) strips for the lower border and side borders and five 2½" (6.5 cm) strips for the binding.

YOU WILL NEED

¼-yd. (0.25 m) bundle of six hand-dyed fabrics in graduated colors.

⅔ yd. (0.63 m) printed fabric.

⅞ yd. (0.8 m) solid-colored fabric, for borders and binding.

1⅓ yd. (1.27 m) backing fabric.

Batting, about 46" × 48" (117 × 122 cm).

Set of triangle quilting tools, such as TRI-RECS™ by Quilt House, for cutting triangles within squares.

Decorative thread.

Beads.

How to Cut Triangles

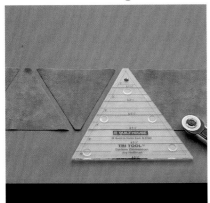

Quilter's tool (wide triangles). Align 4½" (11.5 cm) solid line on TRI TOOL™ with one long edge of 4½" (11.5 cm) fabric strip; cut along angled edges of tool. Rotate tool and align with opposite raw edge to cut second triangle. Repeat to cut additional triangles.

Quilter's tool (narrow triangles). Fold 4½" (11.5 cm) fabric strip in half crosswise, with the right sides together, matching raw edges. Align 4½" (11.5 cm) solid line on RECS TOOL™ with one long edge of fabric strip. Cut along sides of tool to make both a right and left triangle; trim along angle at top. Rotate tool and align with opposite raw edge to cut a second set of triangles. Repeat to cut additional triangles.

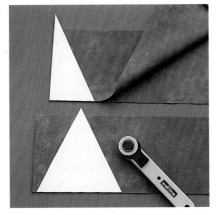

Templates (wide and narrow triangles). Make templates (page 27) from cardboard or template material. Cut the triangles as for quilter's tools, aligning short edges of templates with long edges of fabric; omit reference to angle at top of tool for narrow triangle. Points of triangles extend slightly beyond edges of pieced strips as shown.

How to Sew a Zigzag Wall Hanging

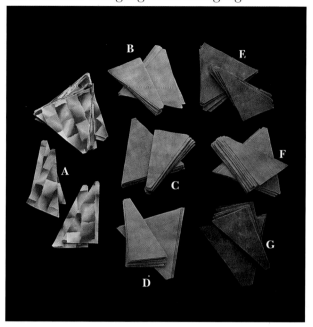

1) Label the triangles of hand-dyed fabrics from B to G, in the desired order (page 27). Label printed fabric Fabric A.

2) Stitch triangles for row one together in order shown in diagram on page 27.

3) Make triangles-within-a-square unit for first unit of row two by stitching a narrow triangle to each side of wide triangle as shown in the diagram on page 27. Continue to make a total of nine triangles-within-a-square units as shown in diagram on page 27. Press seam allowances away from wide triangles.

4) Stitch triangles-within-a-square units for row two together as shown in diagram on page 27. Stitch row two to row one, right sides together.

5) Following the diagram on page 27, continue as in steps 3 and 4 to complete and stitch together rows three to seven.

6) Stitch triangles for row eight together in the order shown in the diagram on page 27. Stitch row eight to row seven. Press quilt top.

7) Measure horizontally through the middle of quilt top and cut a 6½" (16.3 cm) strip from Fabric A equal to that measurement, for the upper border. Also cut a 4½" (11.5 cm) strip from solid-colored fabric equal to that measurement, for the lower border.

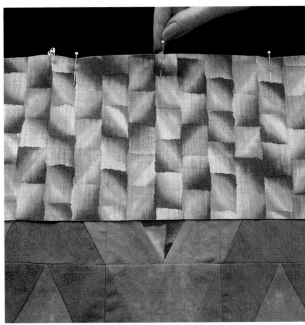

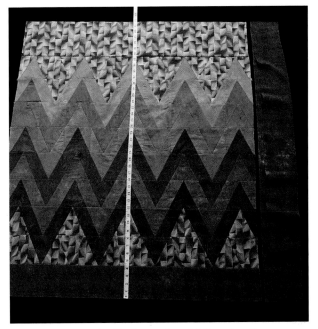

8) Pin upper border strip to upper edge of quilt top at center and ends, right sides together; pin along length, easing in any fullness. Stitch. Repeat for lower border. Press seam allowances toward borders.

9) Measure vertically through middle of quilt top, including border strips; cut two 4½" (11.5 cm) strips from solid-colored fabric equal to that measurement. Pin and stitch to sides of quilt top as in step 8. Press seam allowances toward borders. Cut backing fabric 4" (10 cm) wider and longer than quilt top, piecing as necessary.

(Continued on next page)

10) Mark quilting design lines on side borders of quilt, using chalk or pencil, by extending lines from seamlines of zigzag pattern to the edges of borders. Continue to mark additional quilting lines at top and bottom of side borders 1¾" (4.5 cm) apart; at top, extend markings into upper border.

11) Mark quilting lines in upper border by extending lines from seamlines of pieced triangles in row one. Repeat for lower border by extending seamlines from row eight into lower border. Layer and baste the quilt as on page 117.

12) Quilt by stitching on the marked lines on side borders and continuing to stitch in the ditch (pages 118 and 120) along zigzag pattern in piecing. Stitch on marked lines on upper border, continuing to stitch in the ditch along triangles in row one. Stitch on marked lines on lower border, continuing to stitch in the ditch along the triangles in row eight.

13) Attach fabric sleeve as on page 124, and apply binding as on pages 121 to 123. Stitch beads as desired along quilting lines.

Diagram of the Piecing of the Zigzag Wall Hanging

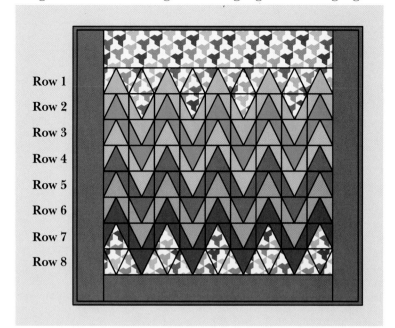

Row 1
Row 2
Row 3
Row 4
Row 5
Row 6
Row 7
Row 8

Color-coded Identification Chart for the Diagram of the Zigzag Piecing

Fabric A	
Fabric B	
Fabric C	
Fabric D	
Fabric E	
Fabric F	
Fabric G	
Border and Binding	

Templates for Wide and Narrow Triangles

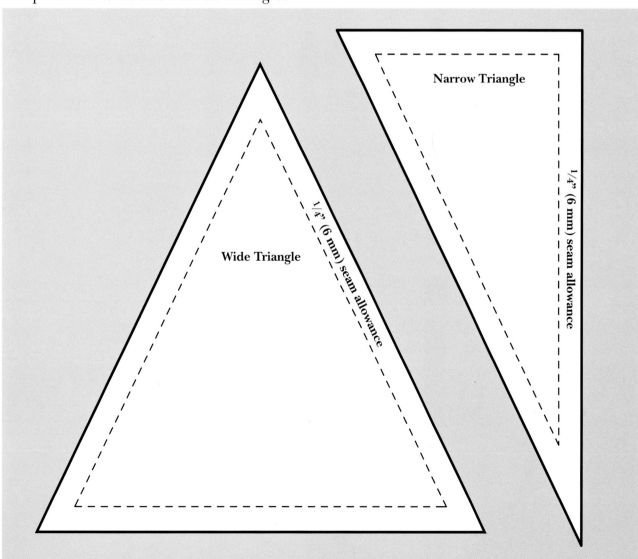

Wide Triangle

1/4" (6 mm) seam allowance

Narrow Triangle

1/4" (6 mm) seam allowance

Trip Around the World Wall Hangings

Create a simple wall hanging with a diamond design in which colors travel diagonally "around the world." The quilt opposite uses hand-dyed fabrics in graduated colors for a bright, bold impression; printed fabrics are combined for a softer look below.

For greater ease in cutting and piecing the small squares that make up this design, eight different strip sets were created. Strip sets are made by stitching strips of fabrics together in a sequence. The sets are then cut to make strips containing squares of each color fabric.

The border of this quilt is embellished and quilted with seed beads. The beads are placed randomly around the border and are spaced a needle's length apart until the entire border is evenly covered. The finished quilt measures about 30½" (77.3 cm) square.

✂ Cutting Directions

Cut one 2" (5 cm) strip across the width of each piece of hand-dyed fabric as shown in the diagram (right).

Cut one 10" × 16" (25.5 × 40.5 cm) block from each remaining piece of hand-dyed fabric. From the 10" × 16" (25.5 × 40.5 cm) blocks, cut seven 2" × 10" (5 × 25.5 cm) strips across the width of each block as shown in the diagram at right.

Cut one 2" (5 cm) square from the excess fabric of color G.

Cut four 3" (7.5 cm) strips across the width of the border fabric.

Cut one 33" (84 cm) square from backing fabric.

Cutting Diagram for Hand-dyed Fabrics

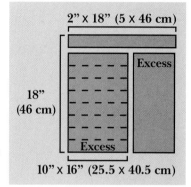

2" × 18" (5 × 46 cm)

Excess

18" (46 cm)

Excess

10" × 16" (25.5 × 40.5 cm)

YOU WILL NEED

¼-yd. (0.25 m) bundle of eight hand-dyed fabrics or eight printed fabrics in a light-to-dark gradation.

⅜ yd. (0.35 m) fabric, for border.

1 yd. (0.95 m) fabric, for backing.

Batting, about 32" (81.5 cm) square.

Metallic thread.

Seed beads.

Trip Around the World wall hanging can be made for either a traditional or contemporary look. Above, a quilt is made from printed fabrics and features silk ribbon embroidery embellishments (page 100). The quilt shown opposite is made of hand-dyed fabrics for a graphic look.

How to Sew Strip Sets for a Trip Around the World Wall Hanging

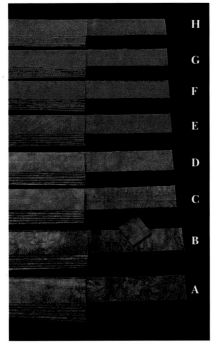

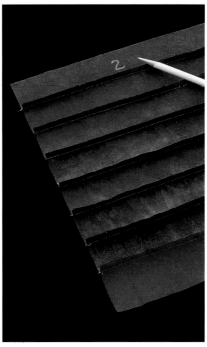

1) Label strips of hand-dyed fabric from A to H as shown.

2) Stitch 18" (46 cm) strips of Fabrics A and B, right sides together, along one long edge. Continue stitching strips of Fabrics C, D, E, F, G, and H to pieced unit in sequence. Label wrong side of strip set with the numeral 1, using a marking pencil or chalk.

3) Stitch 10" (25.5 cm) strips of Fabrics B and C, right sides together, along one long edge. Continue stitching strips of Fabrics D, E, F, G, H, and A to pieced units in sequence. Label wrong side of strip set with the numeral 2, using a marking pencil or chalk.

4) Continue stitching and labeling strip sets as in step 2, beginning with the next fabric in the sequence and starting again at the top of the sequence until eight strips are used. Stitch a total of eight strip sets.

5) Press seam allowances away from the top strip on odd-numbered strip sets. Press the seam allowances toward top strip on even-numbered strip sets.

How to Sew a Trip Around the World Wall Hanging

1) **Trim** one long edge of each strip set at 90° angle. Cut eight 2" (5 cm) strips across Strip Set 1 as shown. Cut four 2" (5 cm) strips across each remaining strip set; keep strips from each strip set together with colors in proper sequence.

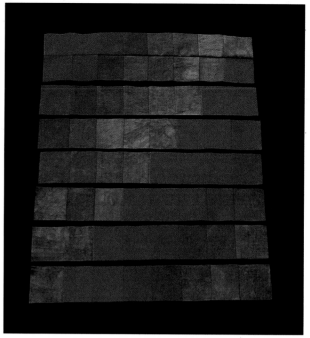

2) **Stitch** strips from Strip Sets 1 and 2, right sides together, along one long edge. Continue stitching strips from Strip Sets 3, 4, 5, 6, 7, and 8 to pieced unit in sequence.

3) **Stitch** strip from Strip Set 1 along bottom of pieced unit. Continue stitching strips from Strip Sets 8, 7, 6, 5, 4, 3, 2, and 1 to pieced unit in that order. Press seam allowances away from middle strip.

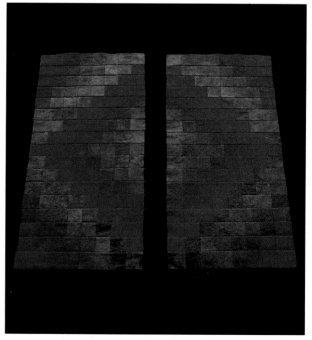

4) **Repeat** steps 2 and 3 to make a matching pieced unit. Arrange units next to each other so pattern resembles diamonds.

(Continued on next page)

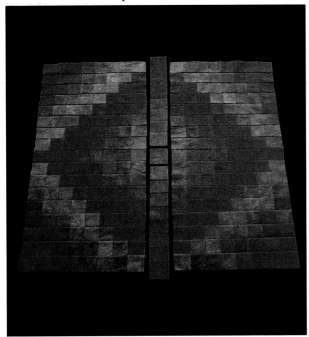

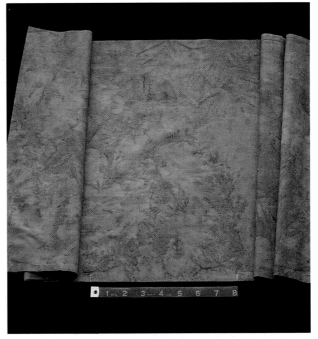

5) Arrange remaining two strips from Strip Set 1 and the 2" (5 cm) square from Fabric G between pieced units as shown. Stitch end of each strip from Strip Set 1 to 2" (5 cm) square to make final pieced strip. Stitch the pieced strip to each side of pieced units to complete pattern. Press seam allowances to one side.

6) Follow page 20, steps 6 to 8, to cut and apply the border strips. Fold backing fabric in half; cut in half along the fold of the fabric. Stitch halves, right sides together, along long edge; leave 8" (20.5 cm) opening in the middle for turning. Press seam allowances open. Cut backing to size of quilt top.

7) Mark quilting lines on each side of the diamond pattern through corners of squares for every other color of diamonds; begin and end lines at centers of squares at diamond points.

8) Place backing and quilt top right sides together. Place fabrics on batting, with backing piece on top; pin or baste layers together. Stitch around quilt top, ¼" (6 mm) from the raw edges. Trim batting to ⅛" (3 mm); trim corners. Turn quilt right side out; press. Slipstitch opening closed.

9) Baste quilt as on page 117. Quilt, using stitch-in-the-ditch method (pages 118 and 120), in seamlines of borders. Quilt diamond design by stitching on the marked lines; pivot stitching at centers of squares at points of diamonds.

10) Quilt border, using seed beads. Conceal the knot of a single thread in batting by piercing the needle through quilt top ½" (1.3 cm) from location of first bead. Bring thread back through quilt top at desired location; pull thread snug, and rub knot with fingernail until it buries itself in quilt.

11) Place bead on needle, and slide to surface of quilt. Stitch through to back of quilt, and make a small stitch; then travel through batting a needle length away from first bead. Continue adding beads in this manner until border is completely quilted.

12) Knot end of thread on the back by winding the thread around the needle, as for a French knot (page 100). Reenter the back fabric through the same hole the thread came out of; travel through batting ½" (1.3 cm) away from hole. Pull thread snug, and rub knot with fingernail until it buries itself in quilt. Attach fabric sleeve to wall hanging (page 124).

Lone Star Wall Hanging with Flower Appliqués

Brighten a wall with this dramatic wall hanging that combines the Lone Star design with dimensional appliqués. The Lone Star design is made from eight hand-dyed fabrics that graduate from light to dark, from the center of the star out to the points. A contrasting fabric is also used to create a circle of interest within the star. The center of the quilt is embellished with dimensional leaves and yo-yo flowers, attached to a vine made from double-fold bias tape. Select fabrics for the leaves and yo-yo flowers that repeat the colors found in the background fabric. The finished wall hanging measures about 43½" (110.5 cm) square.

✂ Cutting Directions

Cut strips from hand-dyed fabrics and insert fabric for the Lone Star design as in steps 1 and 2.

Cut four 11" (28 cm) squares from background fabric. Also cut one 16⅛" (40.8 cm) square from background fabric. Cut the square diagonally through opposite corners in both directions to make four triangles.

Cut four 1½" (3.8 cm) strips from Fabric H, for the inner border. Cut five 3½" (9 cm) strips from the fabric for the outer border. Cut five 2" (5 cm) strips from the fabric for the binding.

Cut ten leaves, using the leaf pattern (page 41), with fabric right sides together as on page 40, step 21. Cut ten circles, using patterns for yo-yo flowers as on page 41, step 24.

YOU WILL NEED

½-yd. (0.5 m) bundle of eight hand-dyed fabrics in a light to dark gradation; or ¼ yd. (0.25 m) each of eight fabrics for Lone Star design and inner border.

⅓ yd. (0.32 m) black or other dark fabric that contrasts with hand-dyed fabrics, for insert fabric.

1 yd. (0.95 m) fabric, for background and binding.

⅝ yd. (0.6 m) fabric, for outer border.

1½ yd. (1.4 m) fabric, for backing.

Batting, about 52" (132 cm) square.

¼ yd. (0.25 m) fabric, for flower appliqués.

¼ yd. (0.25 m) fabric, for leaf appliqués.

1 package narrow double-fold bias tape, for vine.

6" × 24" (15 × 61 cm) plexiglass ruler, for cutting at 45° angle.

Tear-away stabilizer.

How to Sew a Lone Star Wall Hanging with Flower Appliqués

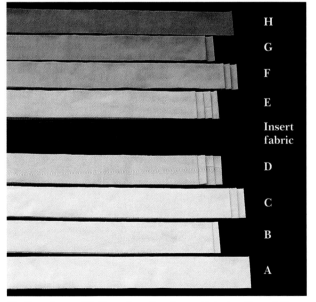

1) Label eight hand-dyed fabrics from A to H, with A being the lightest fabric and H being the darkest. Place Fabric A and Fabric H together, matching raw edges; fold in half. Cut 2" (5 cm) strip across fabrics. Repeat with Fabrics B and G, cutting two strips from each fabric.

2) Cut three 2" (5 cm) strips from Fabrics C and F. Cut four 2" (5 cm) strips from Fabrics D and E. Cut five 2" (5 cm) strips from insert fabric. Arrange the fabric strips in order from A to H, placing the insert fabric between Fabrics D and E.

(Continued on next page)

3) Stitch one strip of Fabric A to one strip of Fabric B, right sides together, along one long edge. Stitch one strip of Fabric C to long edge of Fabric B of pieced unit. Continue to stitch strips from Fabric D and insert fabric to unit in order to make a strip set. Press seam allowances toward lightest fabrics.

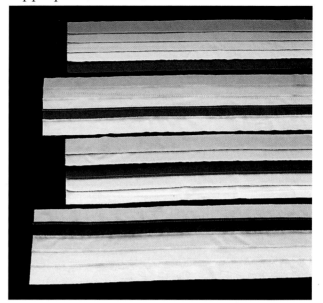

4) Stitch strips of Fabrics B, C, D, insert, and E together as in step 3 to make a strip set. Press seam allowances toward darkest fabrics. Stitch strips of Fabrics C, D, insert, E, and F together to make third strip set; press seam allowances toward lightest fabrics. Stitch strips of Fabrics D, insert, E, F, and G together to make fourth strip set; press seam allowances toward darkest fabrics. Stitch strips of insert fabric, Fabrics E, F, G, and H together; press seam allowances toward lightest fabrics.

5) Cut ends of strip sets at 45° angles, using plexiglass ruler, keeping strips in order stitched in steps 3 and 4. Cut eight 2" (5 cm) diagonal strips from each strip set as shown. After every few strips, check 45° angle and recut edge, if necessary. Take care not to stretch bias edges. Stack strips together and arrange in order as shown.

6) Stitch strip from each stack together in order shown in step 5, pinning strips together at seam intersections; do not press seam allowances open. Repeat to make a total of eight pieced diamonds.

7) Mark wrong side of diamonds where ¼" (6 mm) seams will intersect, placing dots at the wide-angle corners. Mark the wrong sides of background pieces where ¼" (6 mm) seams will intersect, placing dots at right-angle corner of triangles and at one corner of each square.

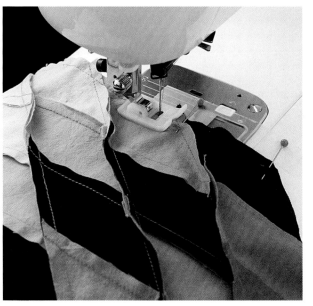

8) Stitch two diamonds, right sides together, along one side, from the inner point of Fabric A to dot, pinning the strips together at seam intersections and finger-pressing seam allowances in opposite directions; backstitch at dot. Repeat for remaining diamonds.

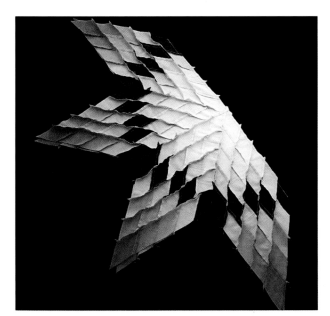

9) Stitch two 2-diamond units right sides together, as in step 8, finger-pressing seam allowances in opposite directions. Repeat with remaining units to make two 4-diamond units. Stitch units together along the long edge, between the dots, pinning at seam intersections; backstitch at dots. Press star carefully, taking care not to stretch fabric.

10) Align short side of triangle to a diamond, right sides together, matching edges at outer point **(a)** and dots at inner point **(b)**. Stitch from the outer edge exactly to dot, with diamond side up; backstitch.

(Continued on next page)

11) Align remaining side of triangle to adjoining diamond, and stitch as in step 10, with triangle side up. Repeat for the remaining triangles, stitching them between every other set of points on the star.

12) Align squares to the sides of diamonds between remaining points of star, matching edges at outer point (**a**) and dots at inner point (**b**); stitch with diamond side up, as in step 10. Align remaining sides of squares and diamonds; stitch with square side up.

13) Release stitching within seam allowances at center of star, so seam allowances will lie flat. Press from wrong side, working from center out. Cut and apply inner border as for outer border of Woven Stars wall hanging on page 20, steps 6 to 8.

14) Measure horizontally through middle of quilt top and cut two outer border strips to that length for the upper and lower outer borders; stitch to quilt top as for inner border. Piece remaining outer border strips together as on page 121, step 2. Measure vertically through middle of quilt top, including outer border strips, and cut two outer border strips for sides equal to this length; stitch to quilt as for inner border.

15) Cut 40" (102 cm) length of bias tape; trim off one fold of tape on narrower side to reduce bulk. Pin tape to center of star, making a wavy circle as shown; butt the ends together. Position tear-away stabilizer, cut larger than design, on wrong side of the fabric.

16) Set machine for short blindstitch, with the stitch width about ⅛" (3 mm); use monofilament nylon thread in the needle. (Contrasting thread was used to show detail.) Blindstitch around bias tape, catching the edge with widest swing of the stitch; remove tear-away stabilizer.

17) Cut backing fabric 2" to 4" (5 to 10 cm) wider and longer than quilt top, piecing with outer border fabric, if desired. Mark center of each side of quilt top and backing fabric with safety pins.

18) Mark quilting design lines on the background squares and borders by extending seamlines of star out to edges of quilt top. Mark quilting lines on the background triangles 1½" (3.8 cm) from the sides of triangle, extending lines into borders. Continue to mark additional lines on triangles 1½" (3.8 cm) from previous markings as shown.

19) Layer and baste the quilt as on page 117. Stitch in the ditch (pages 118 and 120) in the seamlines of the star, from the bias tape out; extend stitching into the borders, following marked lines. Quilt background triangles by stitching on marked lines; begin and end stitching at the raw edge of the border.

(Continued on next page)

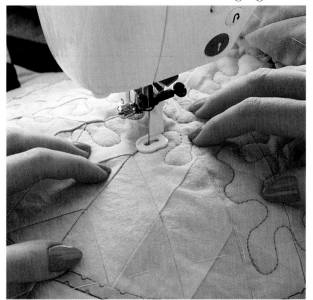

20) Stipple-quilt (pages 118 and 120) the center of quilt inside circle of bias tape. Attach fabric sleeve as on page 124. Apply binding as on pages 121 to 123.

21) Trace pattern for leaf (opposite) onto tracing paper. Fold fabric for leaves right sides together; cut ten sets of leaves, using leaf pattern. Trim some leaves narrower or shorter to vary the shapes slightly.

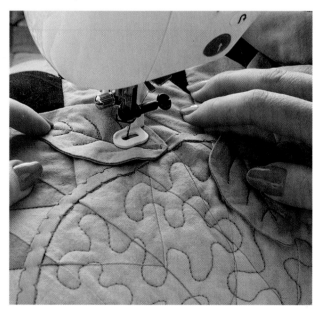

22) Stitch leaves, right sides together, ⅛" (3 mm) from raw edges, crossing over the beginning of stitching at end. Cut a slit in one layer, and turn leaf right side out, using a point tool to smooth outer edges from inside. Repeat for remaining leaves. Press leaves. Transfer markings for veins onto leaves.

23) Pin leaves to bias tape vine, covering the ends of bias tape with one leaf. Stitch leaves to quilt along the vein lines, using free-motion stitching (pages 118 and 120).

24) Trace partial pattern for each size of circle onto tracing paper, placing dotted line on fold of paper. Cut on solid lines; open full-size circle patterns for yo-yo flowers. From each yo-yo pattern, cut five circles from fabric for flowers.

25) Turn ¼" (6 mm) of circle to wrong side, and stitch hand running stitches a scant ⅛" (3 mm) from folded edge. Pull up thread to gather circle, and tie off threads on the inside. Repeat with remaining circles. Pin yo-yo flowers to vine; position button in center, and hand-stitch in place.

Yo-Yo Flowers and Leaf Appliqués

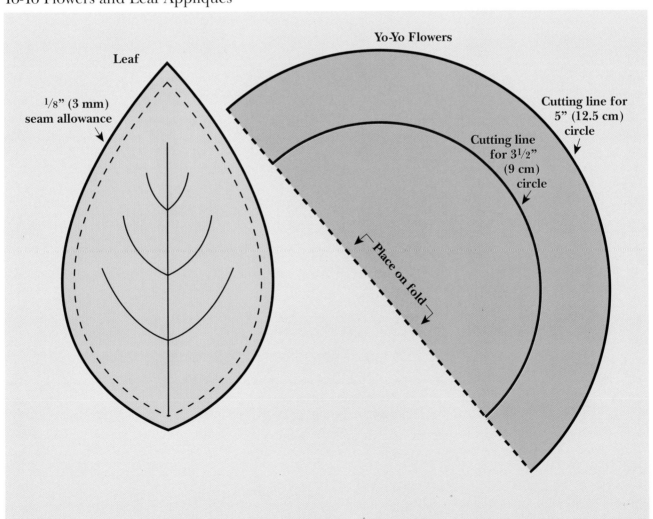

Leaf

Yo-Yo Flowers

⅛" (3 mm) seam allowance

Cutting line for 5" (12.5 cm) circle

Cutting line for 3½" (9 cm) circle

Place on fold

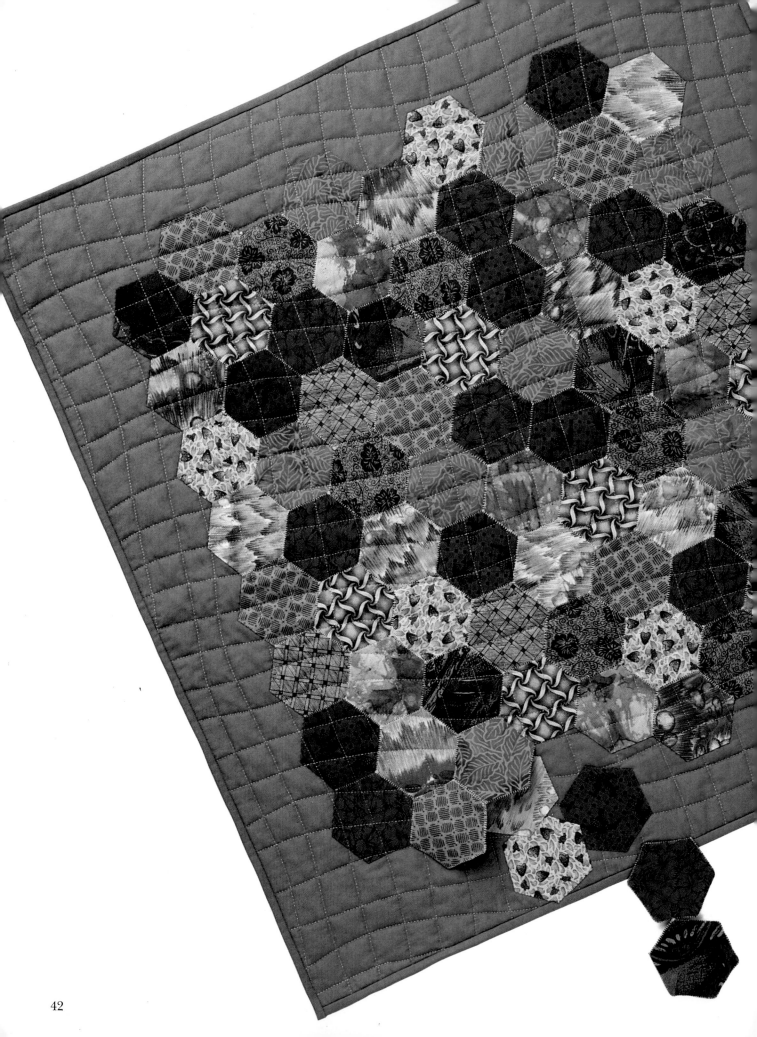

Tumbling Hexagon Wall Hanging

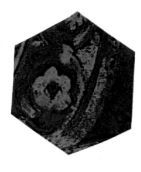

British patchworkers have long used paper piecing for all their designs. Today, it is used for quilt patterns that do not lend themselves well to machine sewing, such as those with no long rows to sew and pieces that need to fit together exactly. Paper piecing is used in combination with machine stitching to produce an accurate, extremely flat quilt top in the least amount of time.

For the Tumbling Hexagon wall hanging, fabric hexagons are first hand-basted to paper cutouts. The hexagons are arranged in any pattern or color combination, then are machine-stitched together, one by one, using a zigzag stitch, which is visible from the front of the pieced unit. The hexagons are steamed before removing the paper pieces in order to keep the hexagons flat and straight.

The hexagons in this wall hanging are arranged in nine rows. Some hexagons are blindstitched to the quilt top as if they are falling away from the rows. Additional hexagons are double-faced and hung loosely on the quilt for a three-dimensional embellishment. The finished wall hanging measures about 26½" × 28¼" (67.3 × 71.7 cm).

✂ Cutting Directions

Make ten photocopies of the hexagon pattern on page 47. Cut the individual hexagons apart.

Cut the desired number of hexagons from each hexagon fabric for a total of 84 hexagons; cut the hexagons ¼" (6 mm) larger than the paper on all sides.

Cut one 27" × 29" (68.5 × 73.5 cm) rectangle from the border fabric.

Cut four 2" (5 cm) strips from the binding fabric.

YOU WILL NEED

⅛ yd. (0.15 m) each of ten or more different fabrics, for hexagons.

1 yd. (0.95 m) fabric, for border and binding.

⅞ yd. (0.8 m) fabric, for backing.

Batting, about 31" × 33" (78.5 × 84 cm).

Monofilament nylon thread.

Tear-away stabilizer.

Decorative thread.

Mediumweight fusible interfacing.

How to Sew a Tumbling Hexagon Wall Hanging

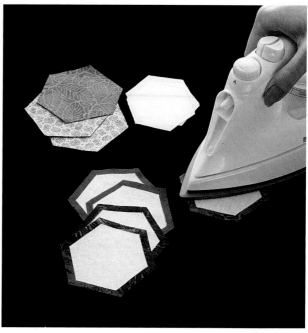

1) Pin paper hexagon to the back of fabric hexagon. Finger-press seam allowances to back of paper; hand-baste the hexagon to paper along seam allowances. Repeat for 75 additional hexagons.

2) Trace paper hexagon onto interfacing eight times; cut out hexagons. Follow step 1 to make eight more hexagons, substituting interfacing hexagons for the paper and fusing interfacing hexagons to the fabric, following manufacturer's instructions. Set aside these eight hexagons until step 11.

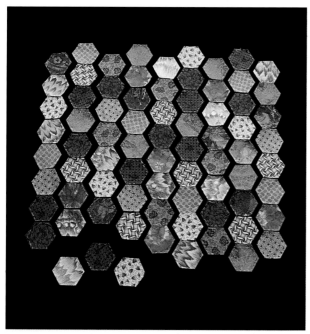

3) Arrange 76 hexagons on work surface in nine columns, alternating eight and nine hexagons in each column, in desired color sequence. Allow a few hexagons in last row to fall away from organized rows, as shown.

4) Stitch first two hexagons of first column, right sides together, using a zigzag stitch with a 1/16" (1.5 mm) stitch length and 1/16" (1.5 mm) stitch width, barely catching the fabric; backstitch at each end. If seam does not lie flat, loosen top thread tension. Repeat to stitch remaining hexagons together in column one. Repeat for remaining columns; set aside individual hexagons for tumbling from last row.

5) Stitch first two columns of hexagons together, one hexagon at a time, as on page 44, step 4. Continue to add columns until pieced unit is complete.

6) Steam pieced unit with paper hexagons still intact. Remove the basting stitches; steam a second time to remove basting marks. Remove the paper hexagons. Repeat with the individual hexagons reserved for tumbling from last row.

7) Pin or baste pieced unit to front of rectangle for border fabric. Position tear-away stabilizer, cut to size of border fabric, on wrong side of border fabric.

8) Set machine for short blindstitch, with the stitch width about 1/16" (1.5 mm); use monofilament nylon thread in the needle. Blindstitch around pieced unit, catching edge with widest swing of stitch. Remove tear-away stabilizer, taking care not to distort stitches.

(Continued on next page)

9) Cut backing fabric 2" to 4" (5 to 10 cm) wider and longer than quilt top. Layer and baste the quilt top, batting, and backing as on page 117.

10) Quilt in long, flowing lines across quilt top in two directions, using walking foot. Attach fabric sleeve to wall hanging (page 124), and apply the binding as on pages 121 to 123.

11) Steam the eight interfacing hexagons. Remove the basting stitches; steam a second time to remove basting marks. Pin two hexagons right sides together; zigzag around five sides as on page 44, step 4. Turn right side out; press. Whipstitch along remaining side. Repeat with remaining hexagons.

12) Hand-stitch individual hexagons to border to appear to be falling away from pieced unit; hand-stitch faced hexagons to pieced unit and to lower edge of quilt.

Pattern for Hexagons

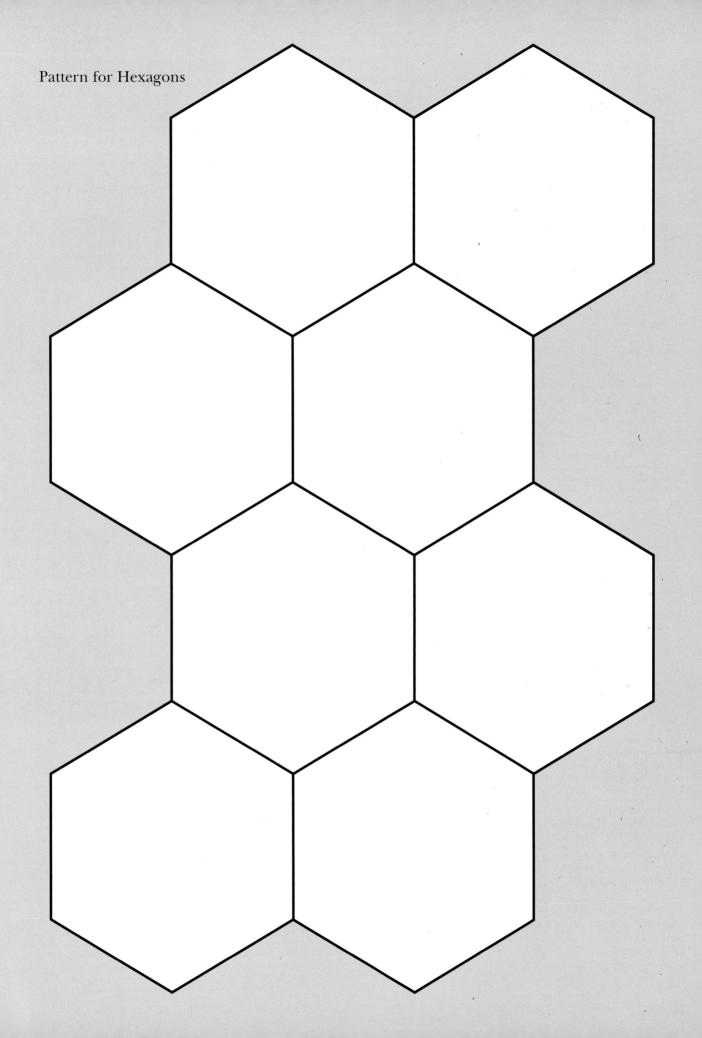

Quilted Landscape Wall Hanging

A landscape quilt made with individual quilt block scenes allows you to incorporate a variety of landscape designs. The quilt blocks in this wall hanging use a number of different techniques to create three-dimensional embellishments. All the blocks combined make a unique scenic wall hanging.

Landscape quilt blocks are assembled separately, then are joined by spacer strips that frame the blocks and allow them to stand out. Quilt blocks and spacer strips are stitched together to make three columns, which can be easily stitched together to make the quilt

top. Individual blocks are quilted according to their own instructions after the quilt top has been layered and basted with the batting and backing fabric. Use a variety of decorative threads for greater interest.

The finished quilt measures about 36½" × 48" (91.8 × 122 cm). The blocks for the Pine Tree, Desert, and Stream measure 12" (30.5 cm) square. The Winter Plains and Autumn Hills blocks measure 9" (23 cm) square. The Seascape block measures 9" × 12" (23 × 30.5 cm). Blocks of the same size are interchangeable in the wall hanging.

✂ Cutting Directions
(for the Landscape Wall Hanging)

Cut two 3½" (9 cm) strips across the width of the fabric for the spacers; cut two 12½" (31.8 cm) lengths and one 27½" (69.8 cm) length from the strips. Cut one 6½" (16.3 cm) strip across the width of the fabric for the spacers; cut two 9½" (24.3 cm) lengths and one 15½" (39.3 cm) length from the strip. Cut four or five 5" (12.5 cm) strips across the width of the border fabric. Cut five 2½" (6.5 cm) strips across the width of the binding fabric.

✂ Cutting Directions
(for the Seascape Quilt Block)

Cut one 10" × 13" (25.5 × 33 cm) rectangle from the water fabric. Cut one 4" × 13" (10 × 33 cm) rectangle from the rock wall fabric. Cut one 5" × 8" (12.5 × 20.5 cm) rectangle from the rock or sand floor fabric. Cut three 1½" × 12" (3.8 × 30.5 cm) strips from the seaweed fabric. Cut the desired number of fish appliqués from the fish print fabric, leaving a scant ⅛" (3 mm) of background around the fish.

✂ Cutting Directions
(for the Winter Plains Quilt Block)

Cut two 11" (28 cm) squares from water-soluble stabilizer. Cut one 5" × 10" (12.5 × 25.5 cm) rectangle from the fabric for the sky. Cut one 6" × 10" (15 × 25.5 cm) rectangle from the fabric for the snow and from white organza. Cut one 6" × 10" (15 × 25.5 cm) rectangle from snowdrift fabric.

✂ Cutting Directions
(for the Desert Quilt Block)

Cut one 1¾" × 22" (4.5 × 56 cm) strip from seven desert fabrics. Cut one 5" × 13" (12.5 × 33 cm) rectangle for the sky. Cut cactus designs from the cactus fabric, using the patterns on page 61.

✂ Cutting Directions
(for the Stream Quilt Block)

Cut one 9" (23 cm) square of water-soluble stabilizer. Cut one 5½" × 13" (14 × 33 cm) rectangle from the fabric for the sky. Cut one 5" × 13" (12.5 × 33 cm) rectangle from the fabric for the background hill. Cut one 7" × 13" (18 × 33 cm) rectangle each, from the fabric for the stream and from the lace. Cut one 3½" × 7" (9 × 18 cm) rectangle for the foreground. Cut one 1½" × 8" (3.8 × 20.5 cm) and one 1" × 13" (2.5 × 33 cm) rectangle from the fabric for the grass. Cut the desired number of fish for the stream. Cut one 16" (40.5 cm) square of tear-away stabilizer. Cut one 10" (25.5 cm) square of water-soluble stabilizer.

✂ Cutting Directions
(for the Autumn Hills Quilt Block)

Cut two 9" (23 cm) squares of water-soluble stabilizer. Cut one 10" (25.5 cm) square from the sky fabric. Cut one 6" × 10" (15 × 25.5 cm) rectangle from the main hill fabric. Cut one 4" × 10" (10 × 25.5 cm) rectangle and one 3" × 6" (7.5 × 15 cm) rectangle from the secondary hill fabrics. Cut one 2" (5 cm) strip from the tulle, for the wind. Cut slivers and small pieces from the leaf fabric, using a rotary cutter.

✂ Cutting Directions
(for the Pine Tree Quilt Block)

Cut one 13" (33 cm) square from the sky fabric. Cut one 6" × 13" (15 × 33 cm) rectangle from the fabric with the pine tree print. Cut two 7" (18 cm) squares from the mountain fabric. Cut one 9" (23 cm) square from the pine tree branch fabric. Cut the moon and trunk appliqués as on page 58, step 3. Cut the pieces for the tree branches as on page 58, step 4.

YOU WILL NEED

For the Landscape Wall Hanging:

1½ yd. (1.4 m) fabric, for spacers, border, and binding.

1½ yd. (1.4 m) fabric, for backing.

Batting, about 41" × 53" (104 × 134.5 cm).

Tear-away stabilizer.

Water-soluble stabilizer, such as Solvy™.

Fine-point permanent-ink marker.

Glue stick.

Monofilament nylon thread.

Tracing paper.

Transfer paper.

Paper-backed fusible web.

For the Seascape Quilt Block:

⅓ yd. (0.32 m) fabric, for water.

Scraps of fabric, for rock or sand floor, rock wall, and seaweed.

Scrap of fish print fabric, for fish appliqués.

Pearlescent beads.

For the Winter Plains Quilt Block:

Scraps of three fabrics, for sky, snow, and snowdrift.

Scraps of shimmery white organza, for snow overlay.

White and silver metallic thread.

Black and white rayon thread.

9" (23 cm) embroidery hoop.

For the Desert Quilt Block:

Scraps of seven coordinating fabrics, for desert background.

Scrap of fabric, for sky.

Scraps of three fabrics, for cactus.

4 mm bright pink silk ribbon and 4 mm and 2 mm yellow silk ribbon, for cactus flowers; chenille needle 20.

For the Stream Quilt Block:

Scraps of fabric, for sky, hills, grass, stream, and foreground.

Scrap of lace, for stream.

Scrap of fish print fabric.

7 mm green silk ribbon.

For the Autumn Hills Quilt Block:

Scrap of fabric, for sky.

Scraps of three fabrics, for hills.

Scrap of tulle, for wind.

Scrap of fabric, for leaves.

Decorative thread, as desired.

For the Pine Tree Quilt Block:

Scrap of fabric, for sky.

Scrap of fabric with pine tree print.

Scrap of dark green fabric, for pine tree branches.

Scraps of two green print fabrics, for mountains.

Scrap of fabric, for tree trunk.

Gold metallic fabric scrap, for moon.

Gold metallic thread.

How to Sew the Seascape Quilt Block

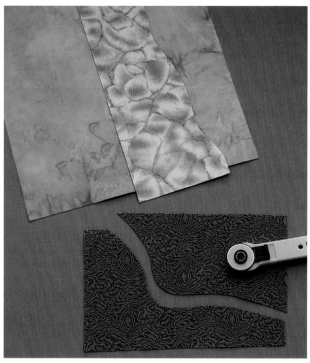

1) **Trim** the fabric for rock wall along long side of rectangle in a wavy pattern as shown; discard excess.

2) **Trim** the fabric rectangle for rock or sand floor diagonally in a wavy pattern as shown; discard the upper half.

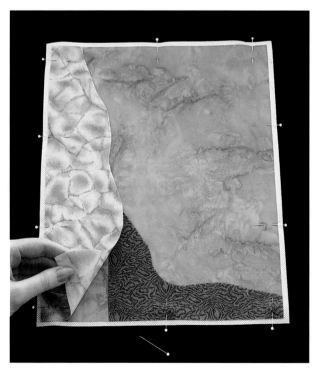

3) **Position** tear-away stabilizer, cut larger than block, on wrong side of water fabric. Pin rock wall to the left edge of rectangle for water, matching long edges. Pin rock or sand floor piece to block, tucking left edge under rock wall fabric.

4) **Pull** several threads from long edges of seaweed strips to fray. Gather and pin one short end of each strip under upper edge of sand or rock floor piece.

5) Twist seaweed strips; pin to water fabric. Stitch floor piece ⅛" (3 mm) from upper edge; do not stitch over rock wall piece. After quilting block in step 4 on page 59, stitch short ends of seaweed strips to water fabric.

6) Glue-baste fish appliqué pieces, as desired, on quilt block; tuck tail of one fish behind rock wall. Stitch around rock wall and fish ⅛" (3 mm) from raw edges of fabric. Trim quilt block to 9½" × 12½" (24.3 × 31.8 cm).

How to Sew the Winter Plains Quilt Block

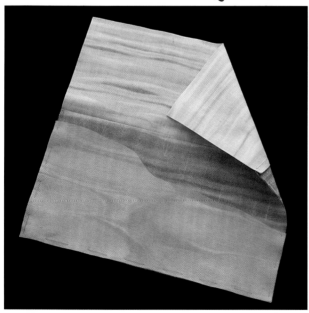

1) Cut curved line on upper edge of fabric for snow-drifts; layer over rectangle of snow as shown. Baste rectangle of organza over these fabrics a scant ¼" (6 mm) from raw edges. Stitch the basted rectangle for snow to the rectangle for sky, right sides together, in ¼" (6 mm) seam. Press seam allowances toward rectangle for snow.

2) Mark trunk and tree branches on piece of water-soluble stabilizer, using a fine-point permanent-ink marker. Pin stabilizer over pieced block, positioning trunk as desired; position tear-away stabilizer, cut larger than block, under block.

(Continued on next page)

3) Attach darning foot (page 120) to machine, and cover feed dogs with cover plate or lower them. With desired thread for trunk in machine, begin free-motion stitching as on pages 118 and 120 at the tips of tree branches with a forward-backward motion. Continue stitching all branches and down trunk of tree.

4) Tear away the excess water-soluble stabilizer, and remove tear-away stabilizer on back side of block. Spray the tree with water to dissolve any remaining stabilizer. Blot block with paper towel; press from wrong side of block.

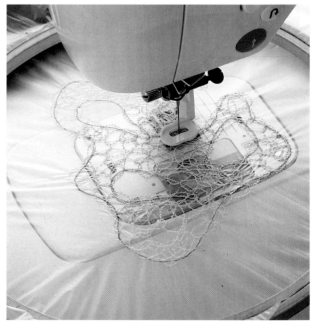

5) Draw desired shape of snow overlay for the tree branches on water-soluble stabilizer. Position square of water-soluble stabilizer over the outer embroidery hoop; push inner hoop into outer one, and tighten. Thread white metallic thread through machine, and wind white rayon thread on bobbin. Position the embroidery hoop under needle of sewing machine, with stabilizer against throat plate and with darning foot in position as in step 3, above.

6) Draw up bobbin thread; holding threads, stitch in place a few times to secure stitches. Clip off thread tails. Using free-motion stitching (pages 118 and 120), make loops or lines of stitching to represent outline of tree branches. Go over stitching several times, making a dense circular cover of stitches. Change thread in machine to silver metallic, and stitch over stitched design again.

7) Remove stabilizer from hoop, and trim off excess. Place stitched treetop design in water until stabilizer disolves; set aside to dry.

8) Position stitched treetop design over branches of tree; position tear-away stabilizer under block. With white metallic thread in machine, stitch treetop to trunk, using free-motion stitching. Remove stabilizer. Trim block to 9½" (24.3 cm) square.

How to Sew the Desert Quilt Block

1) Stitch the seven desert fabrics together lengthwise, using ¼" (6 mm) seams. Press the seam allowances in one direction.

2) Cut 1¼" 1½", 1¾", and 2" (3.2, 3.8, 4.5, and 5 cm) strips across the pieced strip.

3) Stitch the strips together in ¼" (6 mm) seams, staggering strips and alternating widths to make a zigzag pattern about 13" (33 cm) long. Trim off upper and lower edges to make pieced strip 11¼" (28.7 cm) wide.

(Continued on next page)

4) Stitch rectangle for sky to pieced unit along 13" (33 cm) edge, in ¼" (6 mm) seam. Press the seam allowances toward desert. Apply glue stick to edges of cactus design, and position over block as desired. Position tear-away stabilizer, cut larger than block, under block.

5) Stitch ⅛" (3 mm) from raw edges of the cactus pieces. Remove stabilizer. Trim away the excess fabric from behind the cactus designs. Trim block to 12½" (31.8 cm) square. After quilting block on page 60, step 8, embroider flowers on cactus, using silk ribbon as in steps 1 and 2, below.

How to Silk-ribbon-Embroider Cactus Flowers

1) Stitch cactus flower bud **(a)** by making three closely spaced Japanese ribbon stitches as on page 100, using 4 mm pink silk ribbon. Stitch open cactus flower **(b)** by stitching 14 to 16 petals in a Japanese ribbon stitch; leave scant ¼" (6 mm) circle of space at center of petals.

2) Make a three-twist French knot as on pages 100 to 101, steps 1 and 2, in center of the petals, using 2 mm yellow silk ribbon. Make about five two-twist French knots around center knot, using same ribbon.

How to Sew the Stream Quilt Block

1) Cut a curving line along one long edge of the rectangles for hills. Layer lace over stream fabric and cut curve through both fabrics as shown. Cut ½" (1.3 cm) clips close together along one long edge of 1" × 13" (2.5 × 33 cm) rectangle of fabric for grass. Cut 1" (2.5 cm) clips on wider grass strip. Curl longer grass by pulling with fingers as shown.

2) Layer stream fabrics. Stitch scant ¼" (6 mm) from curved edge of stream and hill fabrics. Press ¼" (6 mm) to wrong side along curved edge so stitching is on back side.

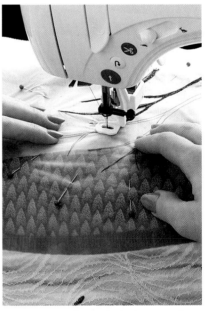

3) Glue-baste fish to stream fabric under the lace. Arrange the stream and hills to form a 13" (33 cm) square, and pin to the tear-away stabilizer. Insert the grass as shown. Glue-baste along the edges to hold pieces in place.

4) Set machine for narrow blind-hem stitch. Using monofilament nylon thread in machine, blindstitch along the curved edges of the hills and stream.

5) Draw tree branch design on piece of water-soluble stabilizer, using a fine-point permanent-ink marker. Position in upper right corner; pin. Follow page 52, steps 3 and 4, to stitch branch design. Trim block to 12½" (31.8 cm) square. After quilting block on page 59, step 5, embroider leaves on branch, using Japanese ribbon stitch as on page 100.

How to Sew the Autumn Hills Quilt Block

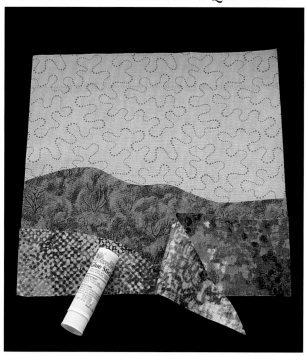

1) Cut curved lines on upper edges of all hill fabrics as shown. Layer background hill fabric over sky fabric. Glue-baste in place. Repeat for additional hill fabrics.

2) Draw shape for tree trunk and branches on water-soluble stabilizer as on page 51, step 2, and mark the position of trunk on hill seamlines. Place tear-away stabilizer under block. Satin-stitch along upper edges of all hill fabrics on each side of position for the tree trunk. Follow page 52, steps 3 and 4, to make the tree trunk and branches.

3) Position slivers of leaf fabric over tree branches, allowing parts of branches to show. Position some leaves on the sky and grass fabrics, as though they are blowing from the tree.

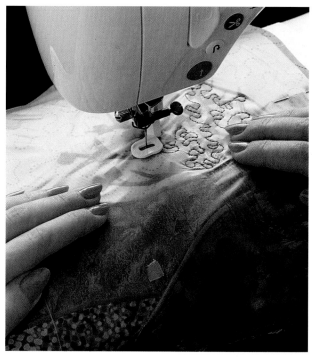

4) Cover leaf fabric slivers with piece of water-soluble stabilizer to hold slivers in position; pin. Stitch slivers to tree and background, using free-motion stitching (pages 118 and 120), catching all slivers with stitches.

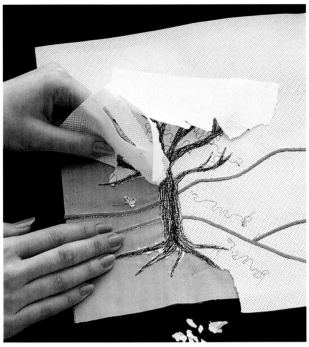

5) Remove tear-away stabilizer, taking care not to distort stitches. Remove water-soluble stabilizer, and press as on page 52, step 4. Trim the block to 9½" (24.3 cm) square.

6) Twist wind tulle strip and position across sky fabric as shown. Hand-baste tulle through center to secure. Remove pins.

How to Sew the Pine Tree Quilt Block

1) Cut curves along the upper edges of rectangles for background hill and mountains. Arrange hill, mountain, and sky fabrics as shown; pin. Glue-baste upper edges of curved pieces.

2) Stitch ⅛" (3 mm) from upper edges of hill and mountain fabrics.

(Continued on next page)

How to Sew the Pine Tree Quilt Block (continued)

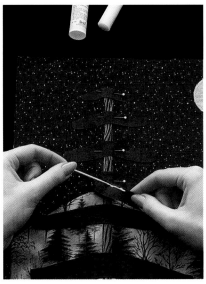

3) Apply paper-backed fusible web to wrong sides of fabric scraps for trunk and moon, following manufacturer's directions. Cut 11" × ⅜" (28 × 1 cm) strip from trunk fabric. Cut 2" (5 cm) circle from moon fabric. Fuse trunk and moon appliqués to block as shown. Stitch ⅛" (3 mm) from raw edges of moon.

4) Transfer six pine tree branch pattern pieces (page 61) onto tracing paper; transfer designs to tree-branch fabric, using transfer paper. Cut pieces from fabric, cutting just inside marked lines. Glue-baste top edges of tree branches to trunk as shown.

5) Stitch tree branches ⅛" (3 mm) from top edges. Clip the bottom edges of branches to create fringe as shown. Trim the block to 12½" (31.8 cm) square.

How to Sew a Quilted Landscape Wall Hanging

1) Stitch 6½" × 9½" (16.3 × 24.3 cm) spacer between Seascape and Winter Plains block as shown to make first column. Stitch 3½" × 12½" (9 × 31.8 cm) spacer between Desert block and Pine Tree block as shown to make middle column. Place 3½" × 27½" (9 × 69.8 cm) spacer strip between first and second column; stitch.

2) Stitch 6½" × 9½" (16.3 × 24.3 cm) spacer on left side of Autumn Hills block. Stitch 3½" × 12½" (9 × 31.8 cm) spacer on left side of Stream block. Stitch 6½" × 15½" (16.3 × 39.3 cm) spacer between the Autumn Hills and Stream blocks to make third column. Stitch third column to right edge of middle column.

3) **Cut** and apply border strips as on page 20, steps 6 to 8. Cut backing fabric 2" to 4" (5 to 10 cm) wider and longer than quilt top. Layer and baste quilt top, batting, and backing as on page 117. Stitch in the ditch (pages 118 and 120) between quilt blocks and spacers and around borders.

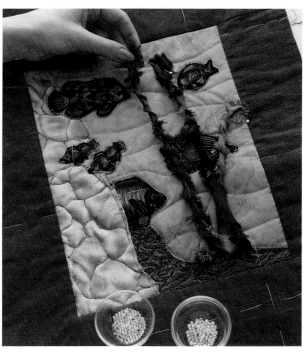

4) **Quilt** design lines on rock wall, rock or sand floor, and water for Seascape block. Stitch beads to block. Stitch upper edges of seaweed strips in place. Brush seaweed to fray edges.

5) **Quilt** Stream block by stitching wavy lines for water and cloud lines in the sky as shown; follow any design lines in fabric, if desired. Stipple-quilt (pages 118 and 120) foreground. Embroider leaves on the tree, using Japanese ribbon stitch (page 100).

6) **Quilt** (pages 118 and 120) Winter Plains block by stitching curving lines in sky and snow as shown.

(Continued on next page)

7) Quilt along rolling hills, close to satin stitching. Quilt around roots of tree. Stipple-quilt sky, catching tulle in place.

8) Quilt wavy lines across sand dune background and sky. Quilt cactus needles for Desert block by stitching with a narrow zigzag stitch; set stitch length to zero. Position cactus needles ⅜" to ½" (1 to 1.3 cm) apart; trim threads about ⅜" (1 cm) long. Embroider flowers of cactus as on page 54.

9) Motif-quilt, using machine-guided or free-motion stitching (pages 118 and 120), upper edges of hill, mountains, and tree branches of the Pine Tree block. Quilt in a zigzag pattern over pine trees on lower hill. Outline moon, and quilt stars randomly in the sky. Quilt mountains as desired.

10) Quilt in desired method (pages 118 and 120) on spacers and border. Attach fabric sleeve to the wall hanging (page 124), and apply binding as on pages 121 to 123.

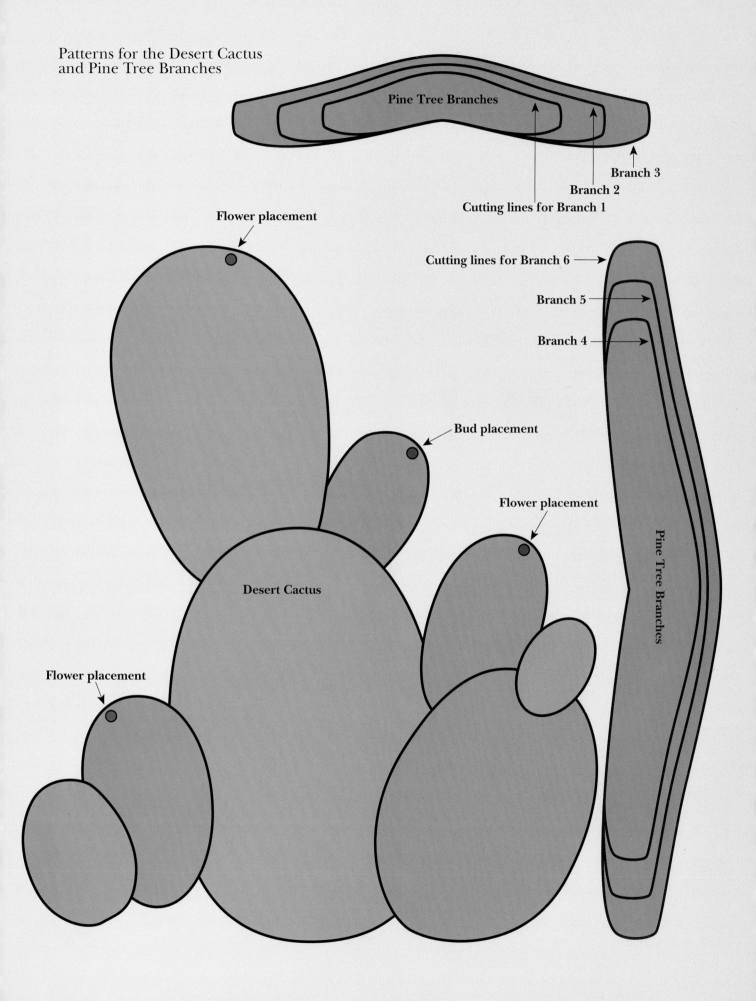

Patterns for the Desert Cactus
and Pine Tree Branches

Pine Tree Branches

Branch 3

Branch 2

Cutting lines for Branch 1

Cutting lines for Branch 6

Branch 5

Branch 4

Flower placement

Bud placement

Flower placement

Desert Cactus

Flower placement

Pine Tree Branches

Inside-out Pinwheel Lap Quilt

Make a stunning lap quilt from pinwheel blocks turned inside out. By stitching the pinwheel blocks with seam allowances to the front side, the lap quilt is given a soft, textured surface after washing. Ties evenly spaced throughout the quilt have frayed edges and add interest to the quilt. Fabrics that look equally good on both sides of the fabric are recommended for this project.

The pinwheel blocks are made from eight coordinating fabrics and one background fabric. The triangle-squares that make up the pinwheel blocks are easily constructed using a paper guide for 3" (7.5 cm) triangle-squares. The guide sheet is first placed over a layer of pinwheel fabric and background fabric. Then you simply stitch on the dotted lines and cut on the solid lines to make several triangle-squares instantly. Triangle-square guide sheets are available at quilt shops, or simply make photocopies of the guide printed on page 67.

The finished lap quilt measures about 42" × 49" (107 × 125 cm).

✂ Cutting Directions

Cut two 9" (23 cm) squares from each of eight pinwheel fabrics. Cut sixteen 9" (23 cm) squares from background fabric.

Cut forty-nine 2" × 6½" (5 × 16.3 cm) strips for the sashing. Cut twenty 2" (5 cm) squares for the connecting squares of the sashing.

Cut five 3½" (9 cm) strips from the fabric for the border.

Cut five 2½" (6.5 cm) strips for the binding.

Cut eight to ten ¾" × 13" (2 × 33 cm) strips on the bias from the fabric for the ties.

YOU WILL NEED

¼ yd. (0.25 m) **each of eight coordinating fabrics,** for pinwheels.

1 yd. (0.95 m) fabric, for background of pinwheels.

1½ yd. (1.4 m) fabric, for sashing, borders, and binding.

⅛ yd. (0.15 m) fabric, for connecting squares of sashing.

¼ yd. (0.25 m) fabric, for ties.

Batting, about 46" × 53" (117 × 134.5 cm).

2⅝ yd. (2.4 m) fabric, for backing.

How to Sew an Inside-out Pinwheel Lap Quilt

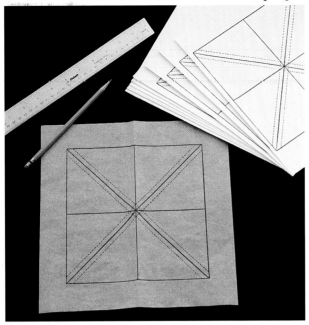

1) **Fold** tracing paper in half to crease; open paper. Trace triangle-square guide (page 67) onto tracing paper, aligning marked line on guide with crease in paper. Turn tracing paper around and trace guide again, realigning marked line on guide with crease in paper; this makes pattern with an X through center. Make 15 photocopies of guide.

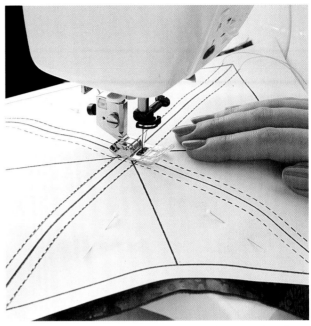

2) **Place** square for the pinwheel and square for the background wrong sides together; pin the paper triangle-square guide on top. Stitch on dotted lines, using short stitch length; thread is visible.

3) **Cut** apart triangle-squares along all solid lines; remove paper. Press seam allowances to one side. Trim off the points extending beyond the squares. Repeat with remaining squares of pinwheel fabric and background fabric.

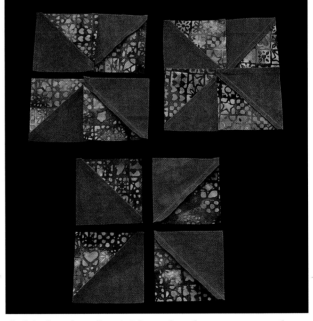

4) **Stitch** pairs of matching triangle-squares together as shown to make a half-pinwheel. Stitch two halves, made in the same fabrics, together to complete the pinwheel block; finger-press seam allowances in opposite directions. Trim off points. Repeat to make a total of 30 pinwheel blocks. Press blocks.

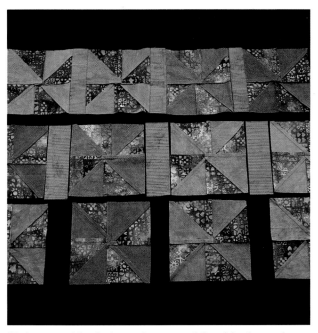

5) Arrange blocks into six rows of five blocks each, with seams on the outside. Stitch the sashing strips between blocks, right sides together, to form rows. Press seam allowances toward sashing strips.

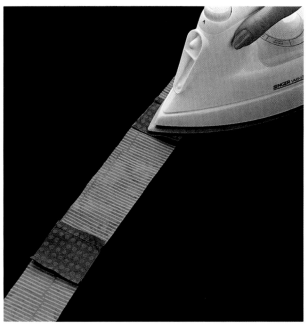

6) Stitch the remaining sashing strips alternately to the connecting squares to equal the length of block-and-sashing row; there will be a sashing strip at each end. Press seam allowances toward sashing strips.

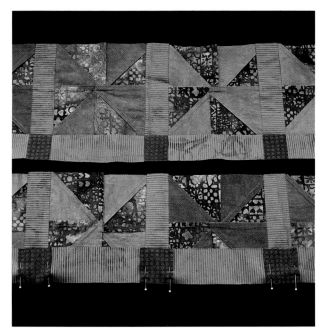

7) Place one sashing unit along lower edge of first block-and-sashing row, right sides together, matching seams. Pin along length, easing in any fullness; stitch. Repeat for remaining block-and-sashing rows.

8) Pin bottom of one row to top of a second row as in step 7; stitch. Repeat to join the remaining rows. Stitch last row of blocks to lower edge of row six. Press seam allowances toward sashing units.

(Continued on next page)

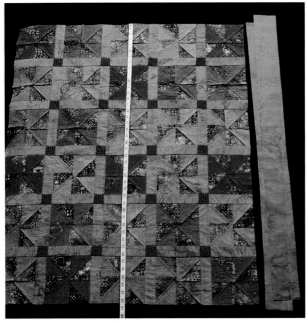

9) Measure vertically across middle of quilt top and cut two border strips equal to that measurement; piece, if necessary, as on page 121, step 2. Pin border strips to sides of quilt top at center and ends, right sides together; pin along length, easing in any fullness. Stitch; press seam allowances toward borders.

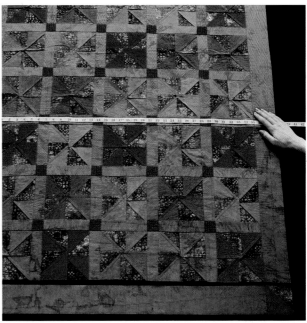

10) Measure quilt top horizontally across the middle of quilt from border seam to border seam and cut two border strips equal to this measurement plus ½" (1.3 cm). Stitch triangle-squares to the ends of upper and lower borders as desired; press seam allowances toward borders.

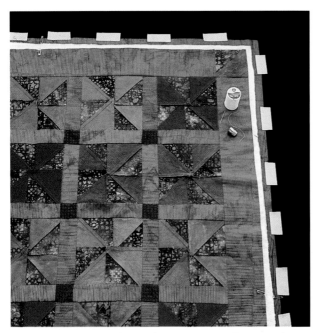

11) Pin upper and lower borders to quilt top as in step 9; stitch. Press seam allowances toward borders. Cut backing and batting 4" (10 cm) wider and longer than quilt top, piecing as necessary. Layer and baste the quilt as on page 117.

12) Quilt in the seamlines of sashing and borders. Apply binding as on pages 121 to 123. Center strips for ties over several connecting squares, spacing evenly over quilt. Secure the ties in place by stitching a straight line across center of each tie strip, starting and stopping stitching a scant ¼" (6 mm) from the long edges; tie in knot. Brush raw seam allowances of quilt to fray.

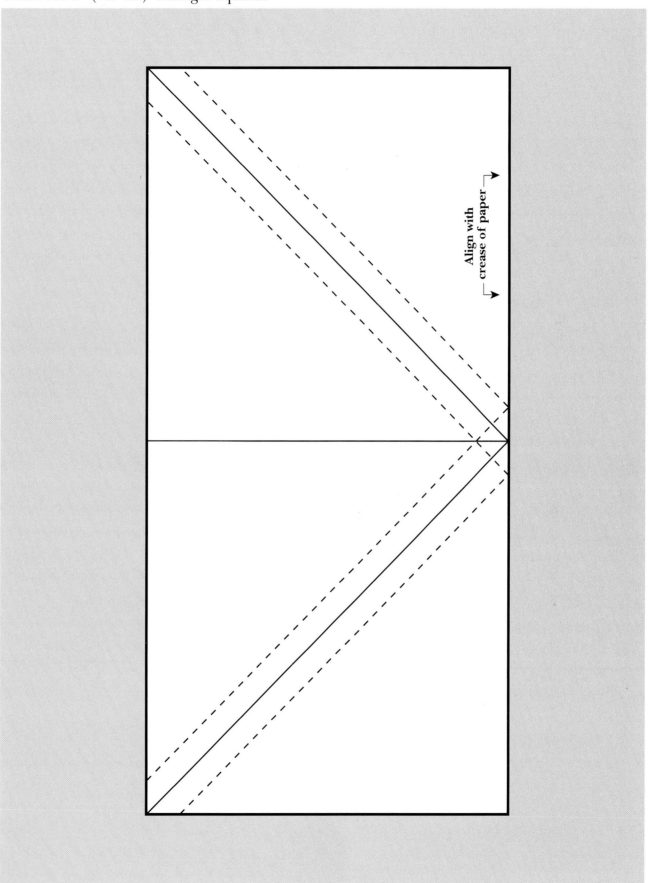

Align with crease of paper

Asymmetrically Pieced Pillows

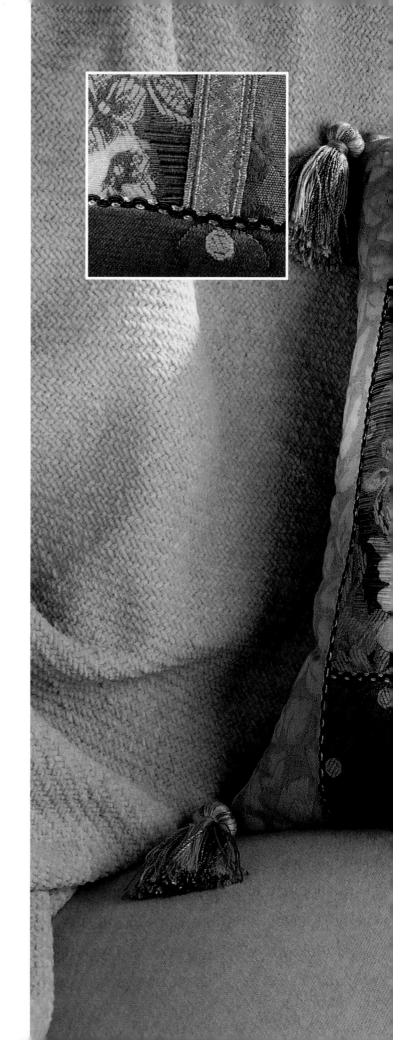

Quilt a pillow to show off your creative flair. This asymmetrically pieced pillow gives you the opportunity to coordinate four different decorator fabrics in a unique way. Select one fabric with a dominant large motif and one fabric with a geometric print. For best results, select fabrics with small design motifs or subtle patterns for the remaining two fabrics. Use one of the four fabrics for the pillow back. The pieced pillow top is embellished along the seamlines, using two widths of coordinating braid trim. The corners of the pillow can be accented with either tassels or dangling beads for additional embellishment. The finished pillow measures 18" (46 cm) square.

✄ Cutting Directions

Cut one 10" × 12" (25.5 × 30.5 cm) rectangle from Fabric A. Cut one 4" × 10" (10 × 25.5 cm) rectangle and one 4" × 19" (10 × 48.5 cm) rectangle from Fabric B. Cut one 7" × 15" (18 × 38 cm) rectangle from Fabric C. Cut one 5" × 16" (12.5 × 40.5 cm) rectangle from Fabric D. Also cut one 19" (48.5 cm) square from one of the fabrics for the pillow back. Cut two 19" (48.5 cm) squares from muslin, for the lining of the pillow front and back.

YOU WILL NEED

Scraps of four coordinating decorator fabrics, including one fabric with large motifs and one geometric fabric, for pillow front.

⅝ **yd. (0.6 m) fabric,** for pillow back.

⅝ **yd. (0.6 m) muslin,** for lining.

Two pieces batting, about 19" (48.5 cm) square.

Polyester fiberfill, for filling out corners.

½ **yd. (0.5 m) flat braid trim,** about ⅝" (1.5 cm) wide.

1¼ **yd. (1.15 m) narrow flat braid trim,** ⅛" to ¼" (3 to 6 mm) wide.

Four tassels, or beads, to embellish corners of pillow.

Diagram of Fabric Placement

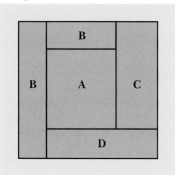

Arrange and label fabrics according to the diagram, using the fabric with the large motif for Fabric A, geometric print for Fabric C, and two fabrics with small prints or subtle patterns for Fabrics B and D.

How to Sew an Asymmetrically Pieced Pillow

1) Stitch the upper edge of Fabric A to lower edge of 10" (25.5 cm) strip of Fabric B, right sides together, in ½" (1.3 cm) seam. Press seam allowances open; trim to ¼" (6 mm). Center and topstitch narrow braid trim over seam on right side of fabric.

2) Stitch the pieced unit to long edge of rectangle from Fabric C, right sides together, in ½" (1.3 cm) seam. Press seam allowances open; trim to ¼" (6 mm). Topstitch ⅝" (1.5 cm) braid trim to the pieced unit, lapping trim a scant ⅛" (3 mm) over seam allowance as shown; edgestitch along both edges of trim.

3) Stitch the lower edge of pieced unit to long edge of rectangle from Fabric D, right sides together, in ½" (1.3 cm) seam. Press seam allowances open; trim to ¼" (6 mm). Center and topstitch narrow braid trim over seam on right side of fabric.

4) Stitch the pieced unit to long edge of remaining rectangle from Fabric B, right sides together, in ½" (1.3 cm) seam. Press seam allowances open; trim to ¼" (6 mm). Center and topstitch narrow braid trim over seam on right side of fabric.

5) Layer and baste the pillow top, batting, and lining as on page 117. Quilt between the pieced fabrics by stitching over braid trim, over previous stitches.

6) Quilt pillow top from the center out, using motif quilting, stipple quilting, or channel quilting (pages 118 and 120), depending on the design in the fabrics.

7) Layer and baste pillow back, batting, and lining. Quilt, using desired technique (pages 118 and 120). If using tassels, stitch tassels to corners of pillow back, within seam allowances.

8) Complete the pillow as on page 75, steps 6 and 7; if using beads to embellish corners of pillow, string beads and secure to corners, concealing the knot on inside of pillow cover before inserting pillow form in step 7.

Diamond-quilted Pillows

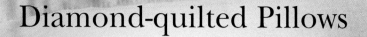

Make this set of coordinating pillows to accent your living room or bedroom. They are made from decorator fabrics and are embellished with tassels, fringe, and beads for an elegant look. The rectangular pillow measures 12" × 16" (30.5 × 40.5 cm) without the fringe. It features a quilted center panel bordered by two side panels edged with flat braid trim. The 16" (40.5 cm) square pillow and the center panel of the rectangular pillow are both quilted in a diamond pattern. Beads are stitched to the points of the diamonds for additional embellishment.

✂ Cutting Directions

For a square pillow, cut two 17" (43 cm) squares from the fabric for the pillow front and back. Cut two 18" (46 cm) squares from muslin.

For a rectangular pillow, cut one 9" × 13" (23 × 33 cm) rectangle from solid-colored decorator fabric and one 11" × 15" (28 × 38 cm) rectangle from muslin, for the center panel of the pillow. Cut two 5" × 13" (12.5 × 33 cm) rectangles from printed decorator fabric, for the side panels of the pillow front. Also cut one 13" × 17" (33 × 43 cm) rectangle from printed decorator fabric, for the back of the pillow.

For square pillow:

½ yd. (0.5 m) decorator fabric.

½ yd. (0.5 m) muslin, for lining.

Two pieces batting, about 18" (46 cm) square.

One 16" (40.5 cm) pillow form.

Polyester fiberfill, for filling out corners.

Four tassels.

Beads.

For rectangular pillow:

⅜ yd. (0.35 m) printed decorator fabric.

⅜ yd. (0.35 m) solid-colored decorator fabric.

½ yd. (0.5 m) muslin, for lining.

Batting, about 11" × 15" (28 × 38 cm) rectangle.

¾ yd. (0.7 m) flat braid trim, ⅝" (1.5 cm) wide.

¾ yd. (0.7 m) fringe trim.

One 12" × 16" (30.5 × 40.5 cm) pillow form.

Beads.

How to Sew a Diamond-quilted Square Pillow

1) Apply liquid fray preventer to the edges of fabric squares, if using fabric that ravels easily. Mark point on one side of square, 1¾" (4.5 cm) from the corner, using marking pencil. Mark point on adjacent side of the square, 2⅝" (6.8 cm) from same corner. Draw diagonal line connecting points.

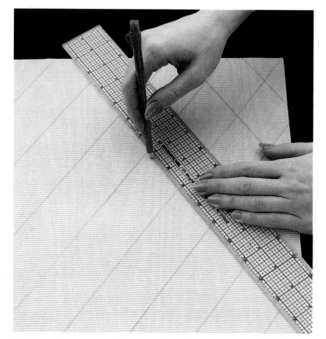

2) Draw lines parallel to marked line, spacing 2" (5 cm) apart. Repeat step 1 on opposite side, drawing parallel lines in opposite direction to make diamond pattern.

3) Layer and baste pillow front, batting, and muslin as on page 117. Quilt by stitching on marked lines, stitching lines in same direction.

4) Repeat steps 1 to 3 for pillow back. Machine-baste layers of pillow front together, ⅜" (1 cm) from edges of fabric for pillow front; trim batting and muslin even with edges of fabric. Repeat for pillow back.

5) Stitch beads to pillow front and back as desired at points where diagonal quilting lines intersect. Stitch tassels to the corners of the pillow back, within seam allowances.

6) Place pillow front and pillow back right sides together; pin. Stitch ½" (1.3 cm) from raw edges, leaving opening on lower edge for turning and inserting pillow form. Trim corners, and press seam allowances for pillow back toward pillow back.

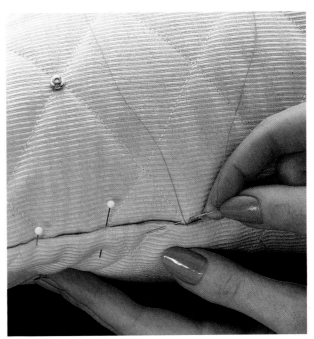

7) Turn pillow cover right side out, pulling out the corners; insert pillow form. Push fiberfill into the corners of pillow as necessary to fill out the pillow. Slipstitch opening closed.

How to Sew a Rectangular Pillow with a Diamond-quilted Insert

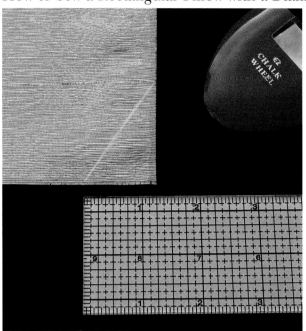

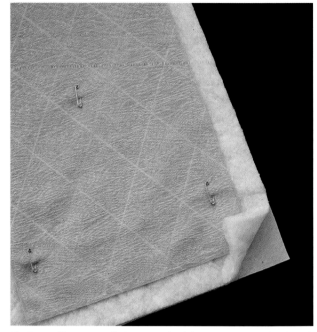

1) Apply liquid fray preventer to the edges of center fabric panel, if using fabric that ravels easily; allow to dry. Mark a point on short side of fabric for center panel, 1¼" (3.2 cm) from one corner, using chalk. Mark point on adjacent long side of rectangle, 1⅞" (4.7 cm) from same corner. Draw diagonal line connecting points.

2) Draw lines parallel to marked line, spacing 2" (5 cm) apart. Repeat marking process as in step 1 on opposite side. Draw parallel lines in opposite direction to make diamond pattern. Layer and baste center panel, batting, and muslin as on page 117. Quilt by stitching on the marked lines, stitching all lines in the same direction.

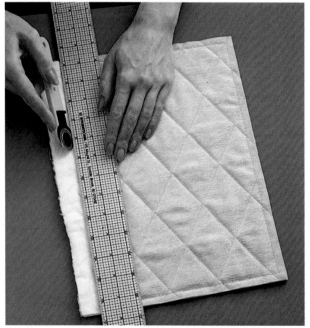

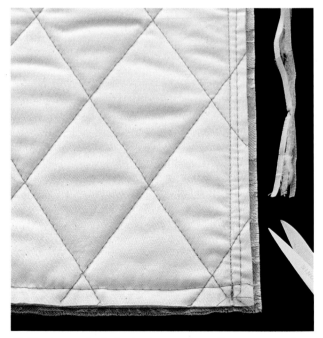

3) Machine-baste layers together, ⅜" (1 cm) from edges of fabric for center panel. Trim batting and backing even with edges of decorator fabric.

4) Center and stitch the long edge of center panel to long edge of side panel, right sides together, in ½" (1.3 cm) seam; center panel may be slightly shorter than the side panels due to shrinkage from quilting. Repeat for other side. Trim seam allowances of center quilted panel to ⅜" (1 cm). Press seam allowances toward side panels.

5) Center and pin flat braid trim over the seam allowances; stitch close to both long edges. Stitch beads to center panel of pillow top where diagonal quilting lines intersect.

6) Apply liquid fray preventer to end of fringe and at intervals of 12" (30.5 cm); allow to dry. Cut two 12" (30.5 cm) lengths of fringe. Center and align lower edge of fringe heading ½" (1.3 cm) from raw edge of fabric at sides of pillow top; allow ½" (1.3 cm) on each end for seam allowance. Machine-baste fringe to the sides, ⅜" (1 cm) from raw edge of fabric.

7) Pin pillow back to pillow top, right sides together, matching raw edges. Stitch ½" (1.3 cm) from raw edges, lining side up, taking one diagonal stitch across corners: leave opening on bottom side for turning and inserting pillow form.

8) Trim seam allowances diagonally across corners. Press seam allowance of backing fabric toward pillow back. Turn right side out; press. Insert pillow form. Slipstitch opening closed.

Maple Leaf Table Runner

Raw-edge appliqués in the shape of maple leaves add dimension and a unique, falling-leaf appearance to a maple leaf table runner. The edges of the leaves can be frayed with a stiff brush, or a more natural frayed look can be achieved after laundering. This more contemporary look gives texture to an embellished quilt. For minimal fraying, use a tightly woven fabric for the appliqués.

Fabric spacers are used on both sides of single quilt blocks to complete every other row in the table runner. Alternating rows are composed of two quilt blocks and no spacers. The spacers are of varying width and add to the unstructured feel of the quilt.

The finished size of the table runner shown is approximately 12" × 42" (30.5 × 107 cm). The table runner can be lengthened by adding additional rows of quilt blocks and spacers. For a wider table runner, increase the width of the spacers and add spacers to rows with two quilt blocks.

✂ Cutting Directions

For the Maple Leaf quilt blocks, cut three 2½" (6.5 cm) squares from each of ten leaf fabrics. Cut two 2⅞" (7.2 cm) squares from each of ten leaf fabrics; then cut the squares into triangles as on page 18, cutting without Easy Angle™ cutting tools. Cut 2½" (6.5 cm) squares from background fabrics for a total of ten squares. Cut three 2⅞" (7.2 cm) squares from each

of six background fabrics and six 2⅞" (7.2 cm) squares from two background fabrics; then cut the squares into triangles as on page 18.

Cut ten 1" × 3¼" (2.5 × 8.2 cm) strips from the stem fabric.

Cut eight strips from the fabrics for the spacers as follows: one 1½" × 6½" (3.8 × 16.3 cm) piece, two 2½" × 6½" (6.5 × 16.3 cm) pieces, two 3½" × 6½" (9 × 16.3 cm) pieces, two 4½" × 6½" (11.5 × 16.3 cm) pieces, and one 5½ × 6½" (14 × 16.3 cm) piece.

Cut seven leaves for the appliqués from leaf fabrics, using pattern (page 81); do not add seam allowances.

Cut four 2" (5 cm) strips from the binding fabric.

YOU WILL NEED

¼ yd. (0.25 m) each of ten fabrics, for pieced leaves.

¼ yd. (0.25 m) each of six to ten fabrics, for background of leaf blocks and for spacer strips.

Scraps of fabric, for appliquéd leaves.

⅛ yd. (0.15 m) fabric, for leaf stems.

½ yd. (0.5 m) fabric, for backing.

Batting, about 16" × 46" (40.5 × 117 cm).

¼ yd. (0.25 m) fabric, for binding.

Glue stick.

How to Sew a Maple Leaf Table Runner

1) Stitch triangle of background fabric to each side of 1" (2.5 cm) stem strip, right sides together. Repeat for remaining triangles of background fabric and nine stem strips. Press seam allowances toward stem strips.

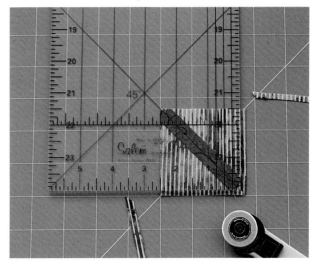

2) Cut 2½" (6.5 cm) squares from each pieced unit, taking care that stem goes through opposite corners of squares.

(Continued on next page)

3) Stitch one triangle from one leaf fabric and one triangle from one background fabric together, along long edge, in ¼" (6 mm) seam. Continue piecing triangles until four matching triangle-squares have been completed for each quilt block, using chainstitching as shown. Clip units apart; press seam allowances toward leaf fabric.

4) Arrange one stem square, one background fabric square, three leaf fabric squares, and four triangle-squares into quilt block design as shown. Assemble block, using chainstitching (page 116); finger-press seam allowances toward center square. Press block. Repeat to make a total of ten leaf quilt blocks.

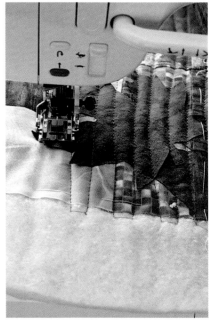

5) Assemble the quilt blocks and spacer fabrics as shown in the diagram opposite. Stitch the blocks into rows; stitch the rows together, finger-pressing seam allowances in opposite directions. Press quilt top.

6) Glue-baste leaf appliqué pieces randomly on quilt top. Cut backing fabric 2" to 4" (5 to 10 cm) wider and longer than quilt top. Layer and baste quilt top, batting, and backing as on page 117.

7) Quilt parallel lines about ½" (1.3 cm) apart across the width of the table runner, catching leaf appliqués in the stitching. Curve lines slightly and switch stitching directions with each line to prevent distorting the quilt. Apply binding as on pages 121 to 123.

Pattern for the Maple Leaf Appliqué

Diagram of Block and Spacer Arrangement

2¹/₂" x 6¹/₂"
(6.5 cm x 16.3 cm)

5¹/₂" x 6¹/₂"
(14 cm x 16.3 cm)

3¹/₂" x 6¹/₂"
(9 cm x 16.3 cm)

2¹/₂" x 6¹/₂"
(6.5 cm x 16.3 cm)

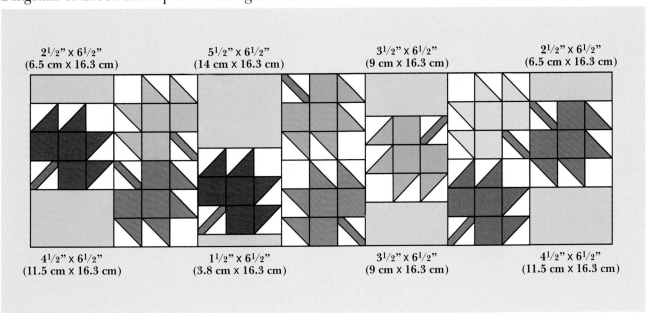

4¹/₂" x 6¹/₂"
(11.5 cm x 16.3 cm)

1¹/₂" x 6¹/₂"
(3.8 cm x 16.3 cm)

3¹/₂" x 6¹/₂"
(9 cm x 16.3 cm)

4¹/₂" x 6¹/₂"
(11.5 cm x 16.3 cm)

Garments
& More

Embellished Quilted Sweatshirts

Brighten your wardrobe with this colorful sweatshirt featuring a pieced design embellished with quilting and decorative beads. The pieced design was created by using paper foundation piecing. With paper foundation piecing, strips of fabric are placed under a paper pattern along design lines, while stitching occurs on top of the paper pattern. After each strip is stitched in place, it is folded back and pinned in place. When the design is completed, the paper pattern is ripped away, leaving the finished design, which measures about 10¼" (26.1 cm) across from point to point.

Make the design from a width of fabric with colors that graduate from one color to the next, or use scraps of six different solid or printed fabrics. With fabrics that graduate from light to dark, use the lightest fabric for the center of the block.

Stipple-quilt the design to the sweatshirt, using decorative thread. Or blind-stitch the block to the sweatshirt, and quilt in the seamlines of the block, extending the stitching beyond the edges of the block to enhance the design. Metallic thread or hologram thread adds sparkle to the design. Coordinating buttons or beads scattered within the design add dimensional interest.

✂ Cutting Directions
(for use with fabric that graduates in color)

Cut four 2" (5 cm) strips from fabric; cut the strips into five equal lengths. You will need four lengths of each of five colors. Label the fabrics as on page 86, step 2a. Cut one 2½" (6.5 cm) square from Fabric A, for the center of the block. Cut one 1½" (3.8 cm) strip from fabric, for the border strips.

✂ Cutting Directions
(for use with scraps of fabric)

Label the fabrics as on page 86, step 2b. Cut four 2" × 9" (5 × 23 cm) strips from fabrics A to E. Cut one 1½" (3.8 cm) strip from Fabric F, for the border. Cut one 2½" (6.5 cm) square from Fabric A, for the center of the block.

YOU WILL NEED

Sweatshirt.

Scraps of six different fabrics; or ⅜ yd. (0.35 m) fabric with color that graduates from one color to the next.

Decorative thread.

Buttons or beads.

Stiff tracing paper or thin typing paper, for pattern.

Monofilament nylon thread, optional.

Tear-away stabilizer.

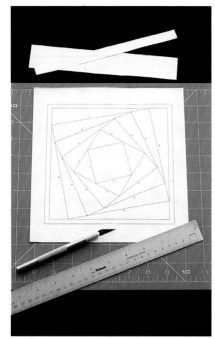

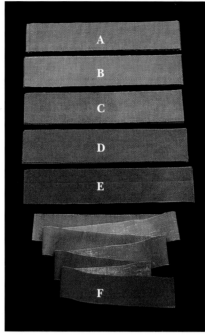

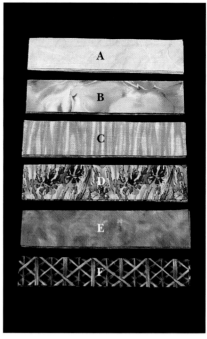

1) Trace the paper foundation pattern (page 89) onto paper, or make a photocopy of the design; trim the paper 1" (2.5 cm) from the outer edges of pattern.

2a) Fabric graduating in color. Arrange and label the fabrics from A to E, labeling fabric closest to the center, Fabric A. Label border strip Fabric F.

2b) Fabric scraps. Arrange and label the fabrics from A to F, graduating from light to dark, labeling fabric closest to center, Fabric A.

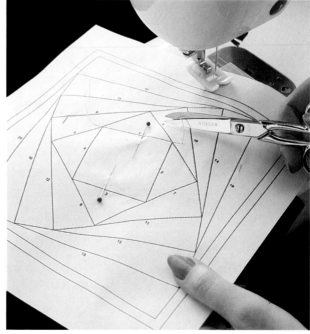

3) Center and pin the wrong side of fabric square from Fabric A to back of paper pattern; edges of the fabric extend ¼" (6 mm) beyond the marked edges of square. Hold pattern up to the light to help in positioning square.

4) Pin strip of Fabric A over center square, right sides together, aligning raw edges on side marked number 1. Stitch with paper side up on line number 1, using short stitch length; extend stitching several stitches beyond line at both ends. Flip strip right side up; pin.

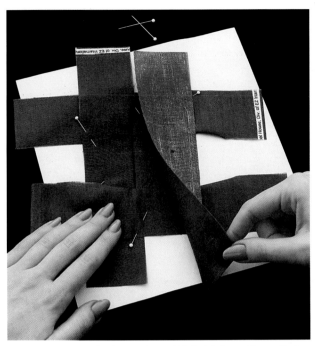

5) Repeat step 4 with strips of Fabric A on lines 2, 3, and 4.

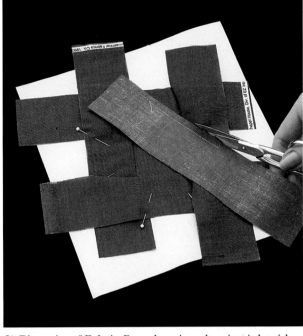

6) Pin strip of Fabric B to the pieced unit, right sides together, lapping strip ¼" (6 mm) over line number 5; hold paper up to light to help align strip. Stitch on paper on line number 5. Trim excess fabrics ¼" (6 mm) from stitching. Flip strip right side up; pin.

7) Repeat step 6 with strip of Fabric B on lines 6, 7, and 8. Continue stitching strips to the block in this manner, using four strips each of fabrics C, D, and E.

8) Stitch on paper around block a scant ¼" (6 mm) from outer marked line on pattern. Trim the excess paper pattern fabric even with outer marked line on pattern. Press 1½" (3.8 cm) fabric strip in half lengthwise, wrong sides together.

(Continued on next page)

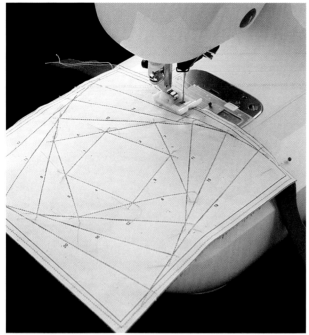

9) Pin pressed strip to one side of block, right sides together, matching the raw edges; stitch on line ¼" (6 mm) from outer edge. Trim off excess fabric strip. Press border and seam allowances away from block.

10) Repeat step 9 on opposite side of block. Repeat on remaining two sides of block, allowing strip to extend ½" (1.3 cm) on each end of block. Press block; remove paper.

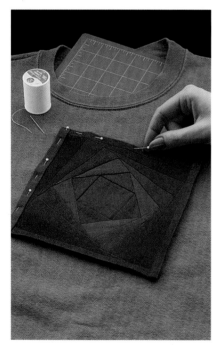

11) Press extended ½" (1.3 cm) ends of border strips to underside of block. Pin block to center front of sweatshirt; baste close to edges of border.

12) Pin tear-away stabilizer, cut larger than block, to inside of sweatshirt, under block. Stipple-quilt **(a)** the block to sweatshirt (pages 118 and 120), using decorative thread; stipple-quilt beyond edges of the block. Or blind-stitch outer edges of block to sweatshirt, using monofilament nylon thread, and stitch in the ditch (pages 118 and 120) in the seams of the quilt block **(b)**; extend stitching between 1" and 3" (2.5 and 7.5 cm) beyond edges of quilt block. Remove tear-away stabilizer. Stitch buttons or beads to block and over quilting lines outside block, for embellishment.

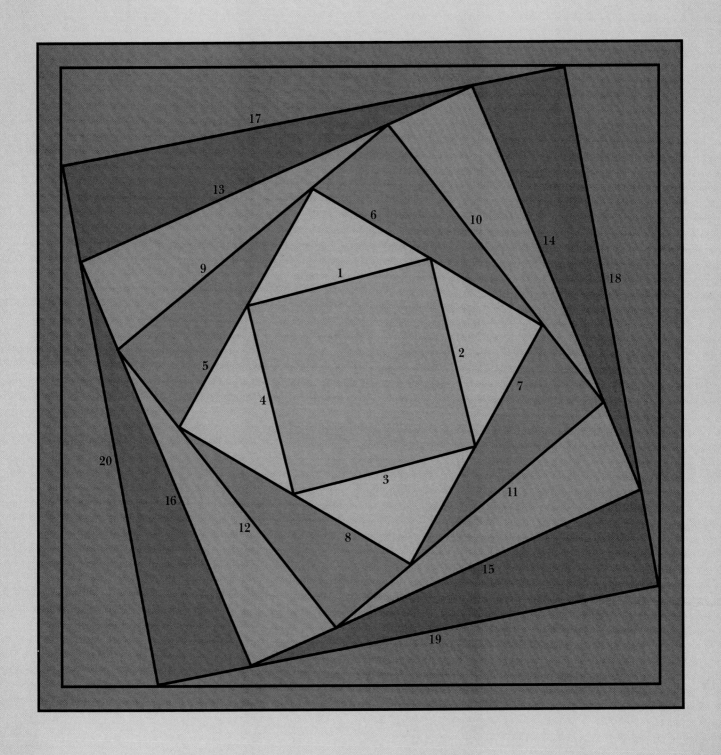

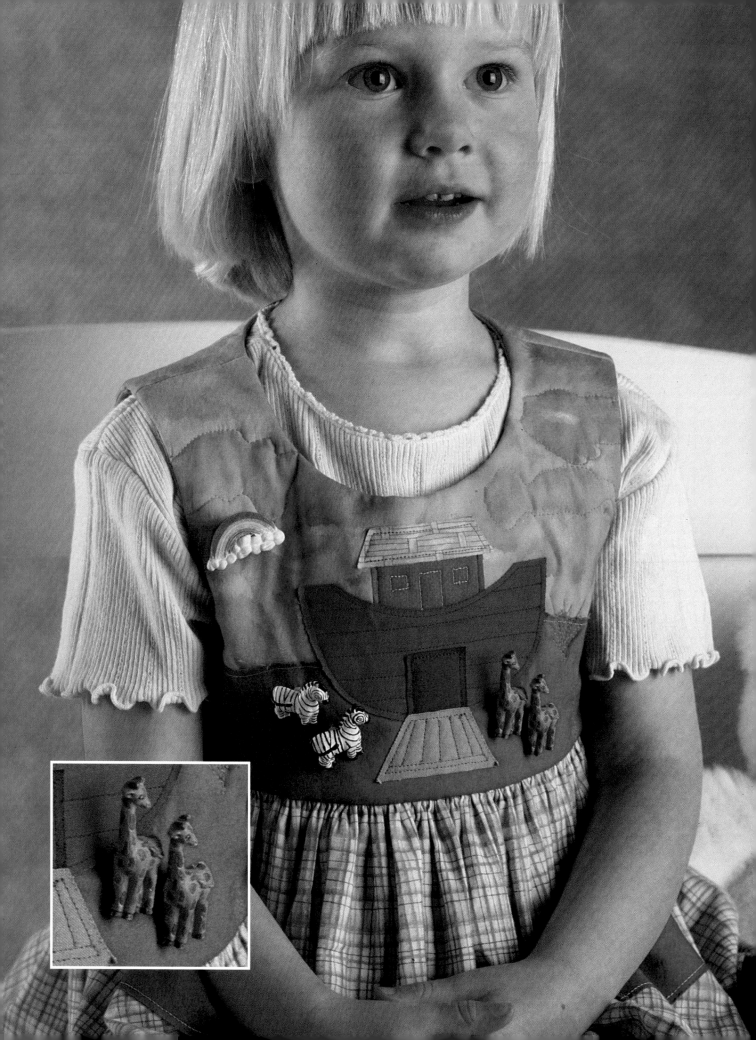

Child's Jumper
with Noah's Ark Appliqué

Create a jumper or romper sure to please any child. Either garment, designed with a yoke, can be used to showcase the Noah's Ark raw-edge appliqué design. Decorative animal buttons add a dimensional characteristic and complete the look.

Select durable fabrics for the jumper or romper, using a contrasting fabric for the yoke, if desired. The Noah's Ark design can be made using scraps of coordinating fabrics. The appliquéd design is applied using a paper-backed fusible web. The raw edges are left exposed and will fray with continued washings, adding a textural dimension to the quilted yoke.

The size of the Noah's Ark appliqué (page 93) can be enlarged or reduced on a photocopy machine, if desired, depending on the size of the child's jumper or romper.

✂ Cutting Directions

Cut the jumper or romper pieces following the pattern directions. Cut the pieces for the appliqué as on page 92, steps 3 and 4.

YOU WILL NEED

Commercial pattern, for child's jumper or romper.

Fabric for jumper or romper, yardage as indicated on pattern.

About ¼ yd. (0.25 m) contrasting fabric, for yoke, optional.

Scrap of green fabric, for landscape of Noah's Ark appliqué on yoke.

Scraps of fabric, for Noah's Ark appliqué.

Batting, two pieces about 12" × 18" (30.5 × 46 cm) square, for yoke.

About ⅓ yd. (0.32 m) backing fabric.

Paper-backed fusible web.

Decorative animal buttons.

How to Sew a Child's Jumper with a Noah's Ark Appliqué

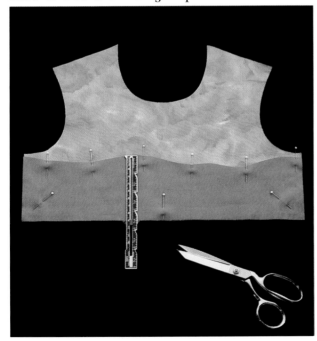

1) Cut 3½" (9 cm) strip from green fabric, with the length equal to width of yoke. Cut a wavy line along one long edge of the strip. Position green strip, right side up, over right side of yoke, aligning long edge of the strip with lower edge of yoke; pin. Trim green strip even with edges of yoke on sides and bottom, if necessary.

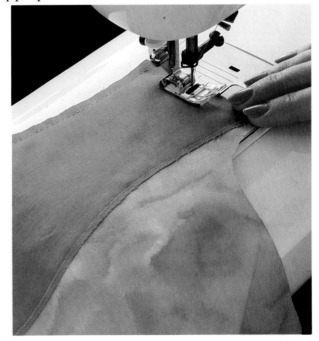

2) Stitch the green fabric in place for the landscape, stitching ⅛" (3 mm) from the wavy edge. Baste ¼" (6 mm) from raw edges of yoke on the remaining three sides.

(Continued on next page)

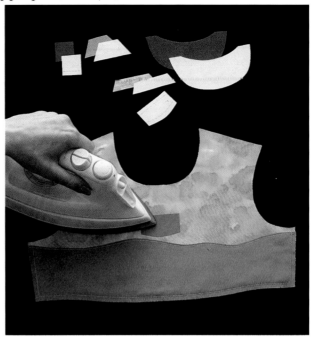

3) **Transfer** Noah's Ark pattern pieces to the paper side of fusible web, adding ¼" (6 mm) to edges of appliqué pieces that go under another piece. Apply paper-backed fusible web to the wrong side of the fabric scraps for Noah's Ark appliqué, following manufacturer's directions.

4) **Cut** Noah's Ark design pieces from paper-backed fabric scraps; remove paper backing. Center and fuse the under pieces of appliqué to yoke front as shown, following manufacturer's directions.

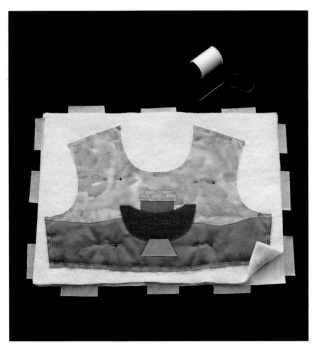

5) **Fuse** upper pieces of Noah's Ark design to yoke front. Layer and baste yoke front, yoke back, and rectangles of batting and backing fabric as on page 117. Baste layers together ¼" (6 mm) from edges of yoke pieces.

6) **Quilt** Noah's Ark design by stitching around the pieces ⅛" (3 mm) from raw edges. Mark interior design lines as indicated on the pattern, using light pencil markings. Stitch on marked lines.

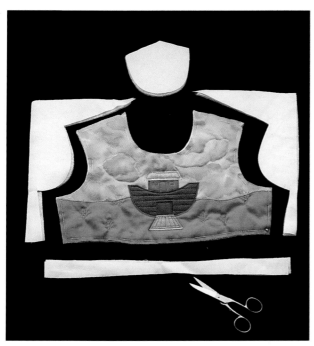

7) Quilt clouds and background design lines, using free-motion stitching (pages 118 and 120). Quilt the yoke back as desired. Trim batting even with edges of yoke pieces. Complete jumper or romper, following pattern directions.

8) Embellish the front of the yoke with decorative animal buttons.

Noah's Ark Appliqué Pattern

Couched Organza Vest

A simple, lined vest can be overlaid with sheer organza and embellished with your choice of a wide variety of buttons and charms to create an eye-popping original. Or choose subdued colors and simple buttons for a more subtle fashion statement.

Basic 2" (5 cm) squares are quilted by couching over decorative thread on the vest front. Buttons and charms are trapped within the squares as it is assembled. The sheer fabric allows the buttons and charms to show through and remain loose. The organza is barely visible, allowing for a dramatic effect, depending on your selection of buttons and charms. For a holiday look, choose an organza with a shimmering finish.

Select a commercial vest pattern for a lined, loose-fitting vest. Avoid fitted vests, because the darts and additional seams would interrupt the quilted squares. Choose a pattern that uses fashion fabric for both the front and back of the vest.

✂ Cutting Directions

Trace the stitching line for the desired pattern size on tracing paper. Add ⅝" (1.5 cm) seam allowances at the side seams and shoulder seams. Mark ¼" (6 mm) stitching lines on the outside and armhole edges. Cut two vest fronts and one vest back from the vest fabric, lining fabric, and batting, using the pattern.

Cut two vest fronts from organza, using the pattern, but add ½" (1.3 cm) on all edges.

Cut binding as on page 97, step 9.

YOU WILL NEED

Commercial pattern, for lined, loose-fitting vest.

Fabric for front and back of vest and binding, yardage indicated on pattern plus ½ yd. (0.5 m).

Organza for front of vest, yardage equal to measurement from shoulder to bottom of pattern plus 2" (5 cm).

Lining fabric, yardage indicated on pattern.

Thin batting, such as Thermore®, or prewashed cotton flannel.

About 62 decorative buttons or charms.

Decorative thread or yarn, for couched grid.

How to Sew a Couched Organza Vest

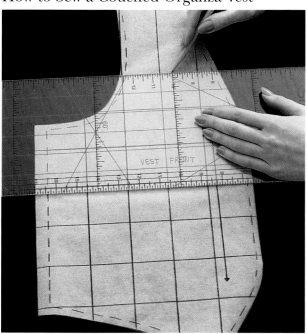

1) Measure the space between side seam allowance and ¼" (6 mm) stitching line at vest center front; then divide by 2. Mark vertical lines as shown at approximately 2" (5 cm) intervals. Place horizontal lines as shown to make approximately 2" (5 cm) squares. Transfer stitching lines on right side of pattern to both vest fronts, using chalk.

2) Mark vertical stitching lines on back pattern at same interval used for front, starting at center back. Mark same vertical stitching lines on right side of outer vest fabric back, using chalk.

(Continued on next page)

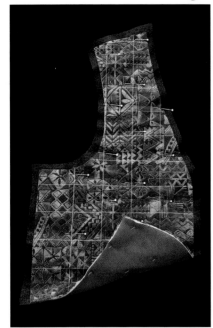

3) Layer the organza, outer vest fabric, batting, and lining for vest fronts; pin in place, using straight pins. Place pins perpendicular to vertical stitching lines as shown.

4) Set machine for narrow blind-hem stitch, using blind hem foot. Couch over decorative thread on vertical stitching lines and one horizontal line across centers of vest fronts. Stitch ⅛" (3 mm) from front edges.

5) Slide charm or button into each vertical channel up to the stitched horizontal line. Fill remaining full squares except those at side seams, pinning on horizontal lines to hold charms and buttons in place.

6) Couch decorative thread on the remaining horizontal lines, enclosing buttons and charms. Stitch ⅛" (3 mm) from the raw edges. Trim excess organza.

7) Layer outer vest back, batting, and lining. Pin as in step 3. Couch decorative thread on the marked vertical lines, using blind-hem stitch. Stitch ⅛" (3 mm) from raw edges.

8) Stitch the shoulder and side seams of the vest together; press to one side. Trim seam allowances to ¼" (6 mm), and finish with zigzag stitching.

9) Lay ½ yd. (0.5 m) binding fabric flat on work surface. Cut fabric in half diagonally. Cut 2" (5 cm) strips from fabric until there are enough strips to bind armholes and edges of vest. Stitch binding strips together as on page 121, step 2; trim. Press binding in half, wrong sides together.

10) Pin binding to lining side of vest, starting near side seam of vest; stretch binding slightly at inside curves, and ease slightly at outside curves. Fold back ½" (1.3 cm) at beginning of strip, and overlap ends about ¾" (2 cm). Stitch binding to vest, ¼" (6 mm) from raw edges.

11) Wrap binding to outside of vest. Pin, covering stitching line. Edgestitch along the folded edge of binding. Apply binding to armholes.

Mitered corners. Apply binding as in step 10. Fold binding as shown, forming small tuck at corner. Stitch binding to vest. Wrap binding to outside as in step 11; mitered fold forms in binding on wrong side of vest. Fold binding into mitered fold at corners on right side of vest. Edgestitch as in step 11.

Quilted Bolero Jacket

This quilted bolero jacket displays silk-ribbon-embroidered designs, wrapped ties, and decorative beads. The jacket uses silk ribbon for embroidery in 2 mm, 4 mm, and 7 mm widths. The wrapped ties of the jacket are made from a bundle of 2 mm and 4 mm silk ribbon, by wrapping the bundle with ribbon from the tassel. The quilted design in the jacket is produced by using a printed fabric for the lining, or backing, and quilting on the design motifs in the print.

✄ Cutting Directions

Cut the jacket and backing pieces from fabric, using the jacket front, back, and sleeve pattern pieces. Cut the jacket front and back from batting in step 1. Cut the sleeve pieces from batting, using the jacket sleeve pattern pieces. Mark the seam allowances and hem allowances on the jacket front, back, and sleeve pattern pieces.

For the binding, cut 2" (5 cm) bias strips.

YOU WILL NEED

Commercial pattern, for bolero jacket.

Outer fabric, yardage as indicated on pattern.

Printed backing fabric, for lining, yardage the same as for outer fabric.

Thin batting, yardage as indicated for outer fabric.

Chenille needle, size 18, 20, or 22.

Silk ribbon, for embroidery in 2 mm, 4 mm, and 7 mm widths.

How to Make a Quilted Bolero Jacket

1) **Stitch** the jacket front to jacket back, right sides together, at shoulder seams. Repeat for lining. Cut batting for jacket front and back, using jacket front and back piece as a pattern.

2) **Layer** outer fabric, batting, and backing, backing side up, for jacket front, back, and sleeves. Pin-baste about every 6" (15 cm), or as needed. Quilt (pages 118 and 120) around design motifs of backing fabric.

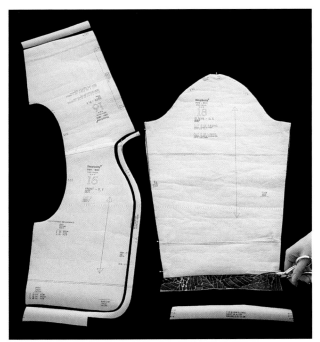

3) **Trim** seam allowances from the center front and neckline of pattern for outer jacket front and around neckline for outer jacket back. Trim lower edges of front, back, and sleeve pattern pieces along foldlines for the hems. Trim quilted jacket sections to match the patterns.

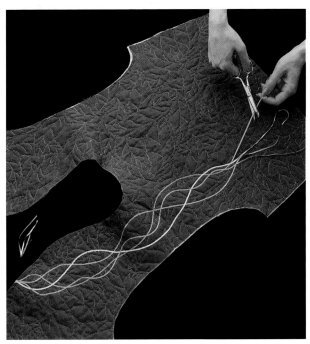

4) **Stitch** several lengths of narrow ribbon in a wavy pattern over the left shoulder, starting ribbon about halfway down jacket back and ending about halfway down center front as shown. Trim ribbon tails in back to about 4" (10 cm).

(Continued on next page)

How to Make a Quilted Bolero Jacket (continued)

5) Stitch jacket side seams and underarm sleeve seams; press to one side. Trim seam allowance to ¼" (6 mm), and finish with zigzag stitching, or serge to finish edges. Insert sleeves, following pattern directions.

6) Stitch binding strips together as on page 121, step 2. Press binding in half, wrong sides together. Follow steps 10 and 11 (page 97) to apply the binding to outer edge of jacket and lower edges of sleeves.

7) Embellish jacket with silk ribbon embroidery (below), using coral stitch to create a wavy pattern and combining Japanese ribbon stitch with French knot to create the buds shown above. Add wrapped silk ribbon ties (page 103) and beads as desired.

How to Silk-ribbon Embroider

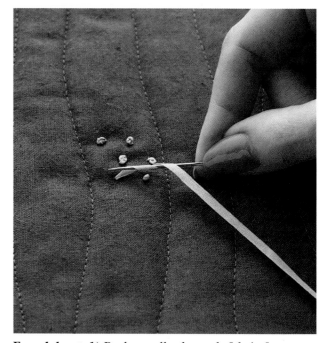

Japanese ribbon stitch. Push needle through fabric from underside at Point A. Smooth ribbon flat; insert needle at Point B. Pull needle through to underside of fabric until ribbon curls at tip; take care not to pull ribbon too tight.

French knot. 1) Push needle through fabric from underside. Holding needle close to fabric at point where ribbon exits fabric, loosely wrap ribbon two or three times around center of needle, taking care to keep ribbon smooth.

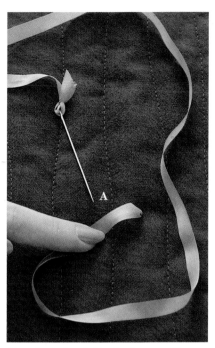

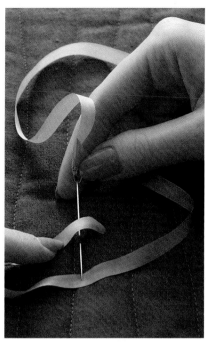

2) Insert needle as close as possible to point where ribbon exits fabric, holding the ribbon in place close to wrapped needle. Pull the needle through to the underside of fabric, rotating the needle as necessary to help work needle through.

Coral stitch. 1) Push the needle through fabric from underside at Point A. Smooth ribbon flat. Make loop, and hold in place.

2) Insert needle to underside of fabric and back up to right side of fabric, inserting needle through the loop as shown. If using quilted fabric, insert the needle through the top fabric only. Pull the needle through the fabric, releasing loop to make a knot.

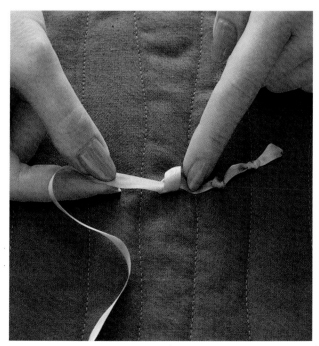

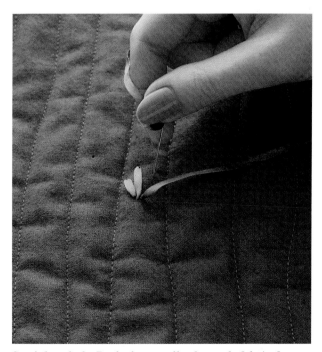

3) Smooth ribbon flat. Make loop and hold in place as in step 1. Follow step 2 to complete second repeat of pattern. Continue until desired length of stitching is complete.

Straight stitch. Push the needle through fabric from underside. Insert the needle desired distance away, and pull to underside of fabric, taking care to keep the ribbon smooth. Repeat for the desired number of stitches.

Tips for Silk Ribbon Embroidery

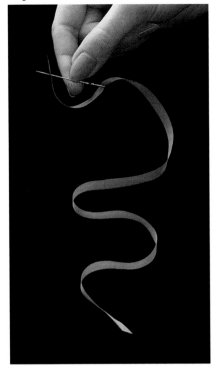 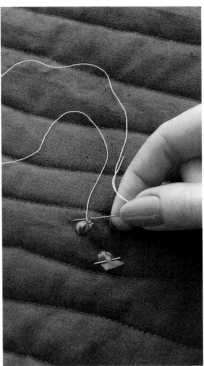 

Thread chenille needle with a length of ribbon no longer than 18" (46 cm). Prevent ribbon from falling out of eye of needle by threading needle and taking a stitch through ribbon near end.

Secure ends of ribbon at beginning and end of stitching with a pin. When stitching is complete, tack ends in place with hand stitching and regular sewing thread; this produces a flat finish with minimal bulk.

Insert needle and ribbon for specific motif between the layers of quilted fabrics for neater appearance on back side.

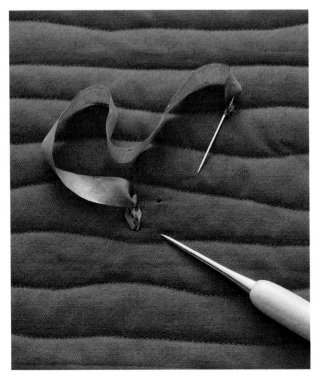 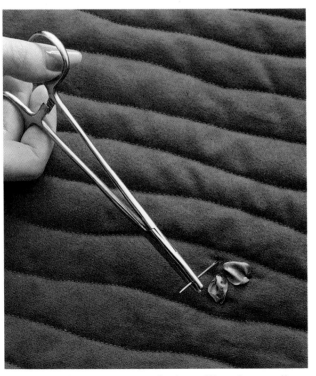

Use an awl to make hole in layered fabrics so wider ribbon can be easily pulled to other side of fabric without damage.

Use a needle gripper to assist in pulling the needle through layered fabrics.

How to Make Wrapped Silk Ribbon Ties

1) **Cut** seven lengths of narrow silk ribbon twice the desired finished length of tie plus about 6" (15 cm) from desired colors. Insert one length into needle; insert into fabric from front side, and pull through to back. Insert needle a scant ⅛" (3 mm) away; pull through to front side. Repeat with remaining lengths of ribbon, inserting into same holes.

2) **Pick** up a length of ribbon, and wrap it around bundle of ribbons near surface of fabric. Keeping wrap smooth, continue wrapping tightly for desired distance. Holding tightly where wrapped, release tail of ribbon back into bundle.

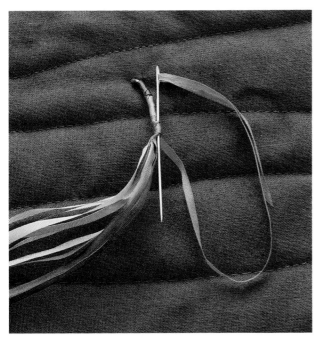

3) **Pick** up second length of ribbon in desired color, and wrap for the desired distance. Continue to wrap additional colors for desired length. Insert last wrapping ribbon through the eye of needle, and insert needle into center of wrapped bundle, along side of wrapping, to take a stitch about ¼" (6 mm) long. Trim end.

4) **Trim** bundle of ribbons to the desired length for tassel, cutting ends at an angle to prevent raveling.

Market Bag

Make a sturdy bag to collect fresh produce from the local farmer's market. This quilted bag features wooden handles for stability. Padded vegetable appliqués embellish the side of the bag and add a touch of whimsy. The vegetables are arranged in a dimensional woven basket pocket, also appliquéd to the market bag. Protect the bag by using a plastic bag as a liner when collecting fresh produce at the market. The finished bag measures 24½" (62.3 cm) across the top, 14" (35.5 cm) across the bottom, and is 16" (40.5 cm) high.

✄ Cutting Directions

For the market bag, cut one 26" × 42" (66 × 107 cm) rectangle from the outer bag fabric, batting, backing, and lining.

For the basket, cut five 1¾" (4.5 cm) strips across the width of the basket fabric. Make fabric tubes for the basket as in steps 1 and 2 on page 105, and cut the tubes to make nine pieces 10¾" (27.4 cm) long and thirteen pieces 7¾" (19.9 cm) long. Cut one 9" × 12" (23 × 30.5 cm) rectangle from paper-backed

fusible web. Cut one 7½" × 10½" (19.3 × 26.8 cm) rectangle from the basket lining fabric.

YOU WILL NEED

¾ yd. (0.7 m) fabric, for bag.

¾ yd. (0.7 m) fabric, for the backing.

⅓ yd. (0.32 m) fabric, for basket.

¾ yd. (0.7 m) fabric, for lining of basket.

Scraps of fabric, for vegetable appliqués.

26" × 42" (66 × 107 cm) thin batting.

Nylon monofilament thread.

Yellow embroidery floss, for corn silk.

Dowel, ⅜" (1 cm) in diameter.

Paper-backed fusible web.

5½" × 14" (14 × 35.5 cm) heavy cardboard, for bottom of bag.

½" × 12" (1.3 × 30.5 cm) strip of heavy cardboard, for pressing template.

Tear-away stabilizer.

How to Make a Market Bag

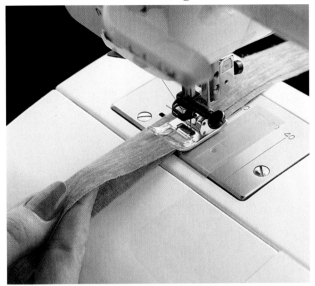

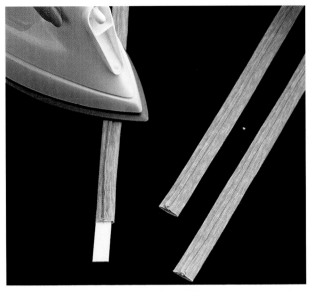

1) Fold strips for basket in half lengthwise, wrong sides together, matching the raw edges. Stitch ⅛" (3 mm) from raw edges.

2) Insert pressing template into fabric tube, centering seam on one side, and press. Move template along tube and continue pressing until the entire tube is pressed. Remove pressing template, and press tube again. Repeat with remaining fabric tubes. Cut tubes as on page 104.

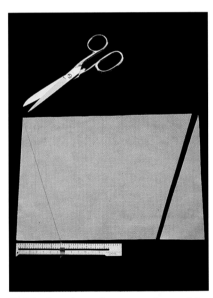

3) Place rectangle of paper-backed fusible web, adhesive side up, on pressing surface. Position nine 10¾" (27.4 cm) tubes for basket strips crosswise over rectangle of fusible web. Place pressing sheet over tubes, and press ends in place to secure; do not press middle of tubes.

4) Weave the 7¾" (19.9 cm) tubes vertically through crosswise tubes. Cover with pressing sheet, and fuse in place, following manufacturer's directions. Remove backing paper.

5) Mark points along one long side of basket lining fabric 2½" (6.5 cm) from the short sides. Draw lines connecting the points to ends of remaining long side. Cut on the marked lines.

(Continued on next page)

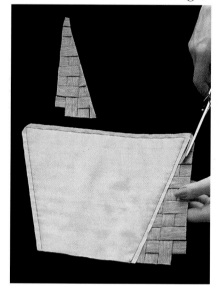 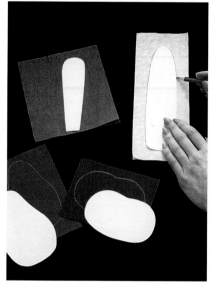 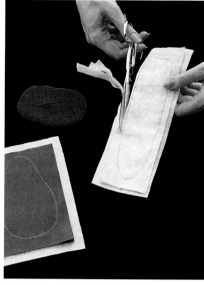

6) Center basket lining fabric over woven strips, right sides together; pin. Stitch ¼" (6 mm) from raw edges of lining fabric along sides and upper edge; trim excess fabric even with raw edges of the basket lining. Turn right side out; press.

7) Trace patterns for vegetable appliqués onto paper. Layer two pieces of each vegetable fabric, right sides together; transfer the vegetable patterns to top layer.

8) Layer vegetable fabric over the batting; stitch on the marked line. Trim seam allowances to ⅛" (3 mm). Cut a slash in the top layer of fabric; turn the vegetable right side out through opening. Press.

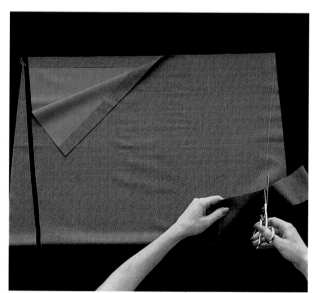 

9) Fold 1¼" (3.2 cm) to wrong side along 26" (66 cm) ends, for facings at upper edges of bag; press. Fold fabric in half crosswise, aligning folds of facing and raw edges. Mark point on fold opposite the facings 3" (7.5 cm) from raw edges on both sides. Draw lines from ends of foldlines for facings to marked points on fold at bottom of bag. Cut on marked lines.

10) Fold the fabric for outer bag in half lengthwise. Transfer pattern for hand opening to tracing paper. Pin the pattern to outer bag fabric, aligning pattern to upper edge and foldline. Cut out hand opening. Repeat on opposite side of bag.

11) Cut rectangles from batting, backing, and lining to shape, using outer bag as pattern. Set aside lining piece. Mark quilting lines on outer bag. Layer backing, batting, and outer bag fabric, and baste with pins about every 6" (15 cm). Channel-quilt (pages 118 and 120).

12) Fold quilted fabric for bag in half, wrong sides together. Place lower edge of basket pocket 5" (12.5 cm) from lower fold of bag. Position the vegetables to appear as if they are sitting in basket; pin in place. Remove basket.

13) Cut several strands of embroidery floss to about 7" (18 cm) lengths. Fold the strands, and tuck under tip of ear of corn to resemble corn silk. Cut 2" × 4" (5 × 10 cm) piece of fabric for carrot greens. Make cuts ¼" (6 mm) apart along one long edge to about ½" (1.3 cm) from remaining long edge. Roll fringed fabric and position under top of carrot, for carrot greens.

14) Appliqué vegetables to bag, using blindstitch appliqué and monofilament nylon thread as on page 39, step 16. Stitch across corn in both directions to create corn kernels. Stitch design lines on carrots and tomato as indicated on patterns.

15) Set machine for a close zigzag stitch, and satin stitch stems on tomato and eggplant as shown. Position basket in place, and pin-mark bag along lower edge of last horizontal basket strip.

16) Remove basket, and turn upside down, wrong side up; press up the excess fabric below last horizontal strip of the basket. Align pressed edge at lower edge of basket to pin marks. Stitch on fold of basket. Flip basket right side up, and pin; blind-stitch along the sides. (Contrasting thread was used to show detail.)

(Continued on next page)

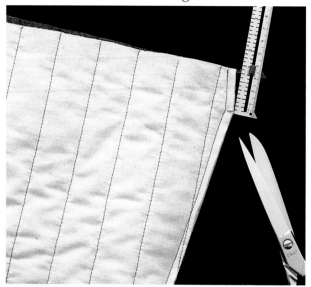

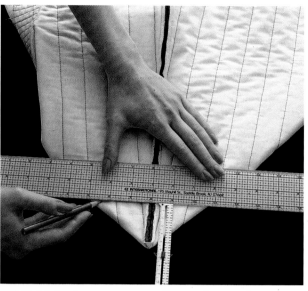

17) Fold quilted fabric for bag in half, right sides together, aligning raw edges. Stitch ¼" (6 mm) from angled sides. Clip the seam allowances at foldline for facing. Repeat with lining piece, leaving 6" (15 cm) opening along center of one side.

18) Fold the lower corners of outer bag as shown, aligning side seam to foldline. Measure 2½" (6.5 cm) from corner along seamline; mark point. Draw line through point, across corner, perpendicular to side seam. Repeat for remaining corner. Stitch on the marked lines. Repeat for corners of lining.

19) Insert outer bag into lining, right sides together; pin around the upper edges. Stitch ¼" (6 mm) from raw edges. Trim corners and clip curves. Turn right side out through opening in lining. Lightly press the upper edges. Slipstitch opening in lining closed.

20) Turn 1" (2.5 cm) to lining side of bag at upper edge for the dowel casing; pin. Stitch close to edge.

21) Cut dowel to make two pieces with 13" (33 cm) lengths. Insert the dowels into the casing through hand opening on each side. Stitch at the ends of dowels, and insert cardboard into bottom of bag.

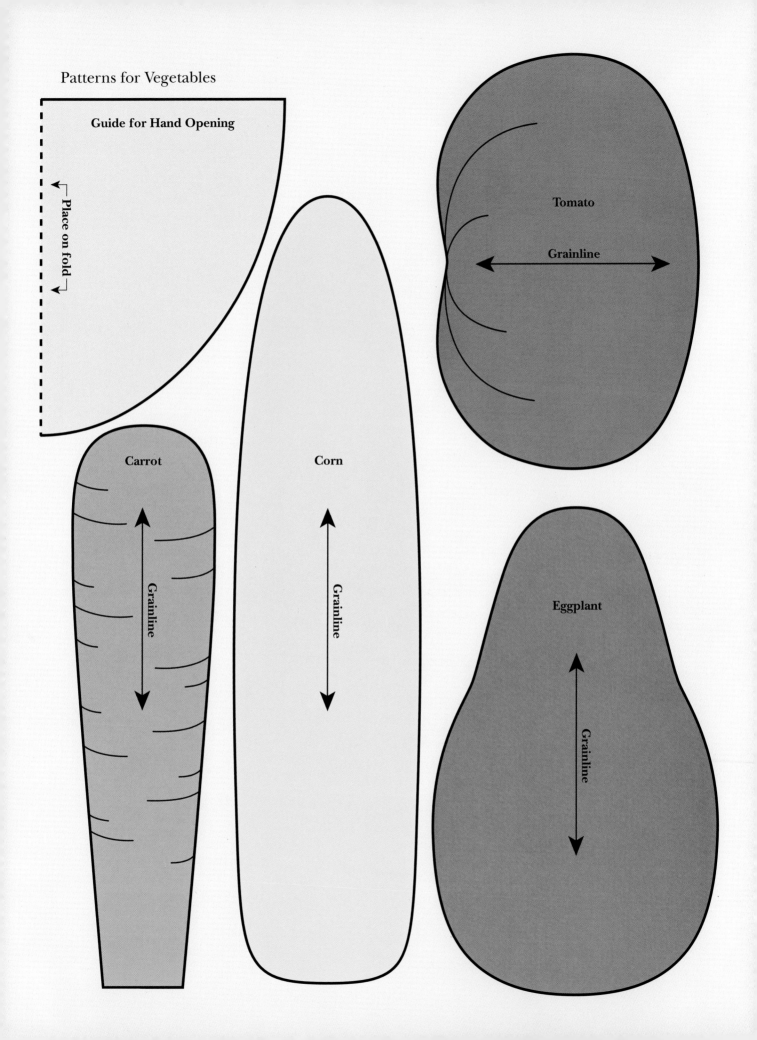

Patterns for Vegetables

Guide for Hand Opening

Place on fold

Carrot

Grainline

Corn

Grainline

Tomato

Grainline

Eggplant

Grainline

Quilt Basics

Fabrics & Batting

Closely woven fabrics made of 100 percent cotton, including calico, muslin, and broadcloth, are the best choice for quilt tops and backings. Cotton fabric is easy to work with and is available in a wide range of colors and prints. Cotton/polyester blends may be used, but they tend to pucker when stitched.

Hand-dyed cotton fabrics in solid graduating colors are available in packets of six or eight "fat quarters," which measure about 18" (46 cm) square. Half-yard (0.5 m) and 1-yard (0.95 m) bundles of hand-dyed fabrics are also available and measure the full width of the fabric. These packets of fabric contain either gradations of a single color or gradations that form a bridge from one color to another. Hand-dyed fabrics are especially suitable for making quilts with subtle blends of colors or for creating a tone-on-tone effect. These hand-dyed packets are available from quilting stores and mail-order suppliers.

Selection of the quilt backing fabric depends on the end use of the quilt. For wall hangings, where the backing fabric is not visible, an inexpensive fabric such as muslin can be used. For a lap quilt, you may want to select a solid-colored or printed fabric to coordinate with the quilt top. A solid-colored fabric accentuates the quilting stitches, while a printed fabric tends to hide them. To create added interest on the back of a quilt, the backing can be pieced, using leftover lengths of fabric from the quilt top. When seaming the backing fabric, trim away the selvages before stitching.

Rinse washable fabrics in warm water to preshrink them and remove any sizing. Check the rinse water of dark or vivid fabrics to be sure they are colorfast; if dye transfers to the water, continue rinsing the fabric until the water is clear. Machine dry the fabric until it is only slightly damp, and then press it.

Batting is available in a variety of types and is usually made of polyester, cotton, or cotton/polyester. When batting is selected for a specific project, the amount of loft in the batting, its drapability, and the distance between quilting stitches are major considerations. Follow the manufacturer's recommendations for the minimum distance between quilting stitches. This distance usually ranges from 1" to 6" (2.5 to 15 cm).

Low-loft battings are recommended for machine quilting; but even low-loft battings vary in thickness. Extra-low-loft battings are often used for garments. For most wall hangings or lap quilts, select a low-loft batting that is sturdy, but has some drapability. Follow the manufacturer's recommendations for pretreating the batting. Some battings must be rinsed or washed with soap before they are used. The battings shown at left are good choices for the machine-quilted projects in this book. From top to bottom are cotton/polyester blends (**a** and **b**) and extra-low-loft polyester batting (**c**).

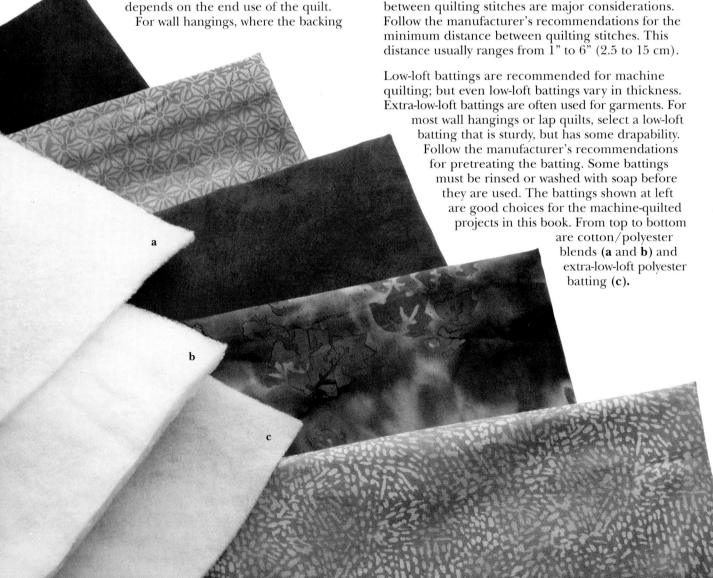

Timesaving Cutting Techniques

The projects in this book are made easily with the use of quick cutting techniques. Most pieces can be cut quickly and accurately using a rotary cutter, a cutting mat, and a clear plastic ruler. It is not necessary to straighten quilting fabrics that are off-grain or to find the grainline by pulling threads or tearing the fabric.

All pieces, including borders, sashing, and binding, are cut on the crosswise grain unless otherwise specified. Strips are cut across the width of the fabric; then the strips are cut into the required pieces. Most of the pieces can be cut using a wide, see-through quilting ruler. Tape thin strips of fine sandpaper across the bottom of see-through rulers, using double-stick tape, to prevent the ruler from slipping when you are cutting the fabric. To ensure accurate measurements for the sashing, borders, and binding, these strips are usually cut after the quilt top is completed.

Some projects in this book use a quilter's tool or template as a guide for cutting the pieces. Template patterns and instructions for making templates are included with the specific projects.

How to Cut Fabric Using Timesaving Cutting Techniques

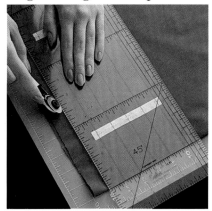

1) Fold the fabric in half, selvages together. Hold the selvage edges, letting the fold hang free. Shift one side of the fabric until fold hangs straight. Foldline is on the straight of grain.

2) Lay fabric on cutting mat, with fold along a grid line. Place ruler on fabric close to raw edge at 90° angle to fold. Trim along edge of the ruler, taking care not to move the fabric.

3) Place ruler on fabric, aligning trimmed edge with measurement on ruler; cut along edge of ruler. After cutting several strips, check fabric to be sure cut edge is still at 90° angle to fold, as in step 2.

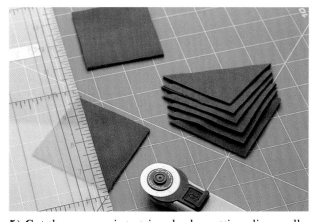

4) Cut squares and rectangles from strips; three or four strips may be stacked with the edges matching exactly. Place the ruler on fabric near selvages at 90° angle to long edges of strips. Trim off selvages. Place ruler on fabric, aligning short edge of fabric with the measurement on ruler. Cut, holding ruler firmly.

5) Cut the squares into triangles by cutting diagonally through each square; cut once or twice diagonally, following the cutting directions for the specific project. Three or four squares may be stacked, matching the edges exactly.

Basic Piecing Techniques

The projects in this book are made using quick and easy piecing techniques and allow for ¼" (6 mm) seam allowances unless otherwise specified. Accurate stitching is critical to successful piecing. It is important to stitch seams exactly, with matching corners and points. A small error can multiply itself many times, resulting in a block or quilt that does not fit together properly.

If you have a seam guide on your sewing machine, check the placement of the ¼" (6 mm) mark by stitching on a scrap of fabric. If your machine does not have a seam guide, mark one on the bed of the machine with tape. To check your stitching, measure a completed block to be sure it is the proper size. The measurement of the block should equal the desired finished size plus ½" (1.3 cm) for ¼" (6 mm) seam allowances on the sides. To achieve the correct finished block size, it may be necessary to stitch scant ¼" (6 mm) seams to allow for the turn of the cloth or shrinkage due to multiple seams.

To save time, use chainstitching whenever possible, stitching pieces together without backstitching or stopping between the pieces. Then remove the chain of units and clip the connecting threads. For secure

Stitch intersecting seams with the seam allowances finger-pressed in opposite directions, to distribute the bulk evenly.

Trim off any points that extend beyond the edges of a block or unit. This eliminates unnecessary bulk and allows for smooth stitching during quilting.

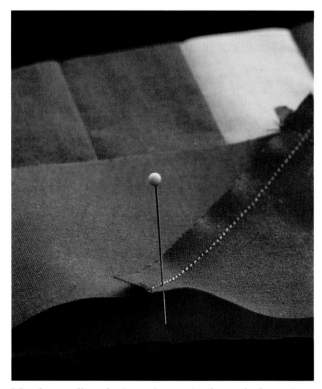

Match seamlines by inserting a pin through the points where the seamlines should meet; remove the pin as you come to it.

stitching without any backstitching, stitch the pieces together using a stitch length of about 15 stitches per inch (2.5 cm). Quilt blocks composed of several units, or squares, can also be assembled using chainstitching. This method is helpful in keeping the units of a block in the proper arrangement.

When you are stitching, take care to keep the thread tensions even, and check to see that the fabric does not pucker when stitched. Match the thread color to the darker fabric, or use a neutral thread color, such as ivory, black, or gray, that will blend with all of the fabrics in the quilt.

When piecing a quilt, press the seams to one side. It is best to press them to the darker fabric to prevent show-through. Because pressing with an iron can distort bias seams, the seams are finger-pressed until a quilt block or unit has straight of grain on all four sides.

To prevent seam imprints on the right side of the quilt, press the quilt blocks or units lightly, using a steam iron. Press them first from the wrong side; then press them again from the right side. The quilt should not be pressed after it is completed, because pressing would flatten the batting.

Stitch through the center of the "X" formed by pieced triangles, to make sure the points of the triangles are complete.

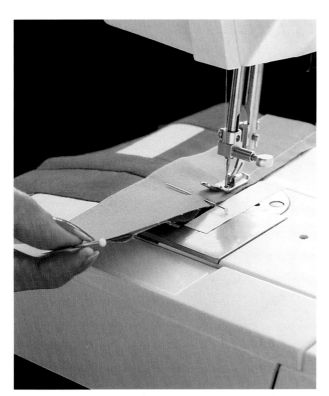

Pin pieces of slightly different lengths together, matching ends. Stitch with longer piece on bottom, easing in excess fullness.

Finger-press bias seams to avoid distorting them. Press with an iron only after unit or quilt block has straight of grain on all four sides.

How to Assemble a Quilt Block Using Chainstitching

1) **Arrange** quilt block units into desired arrangement. Stitch first two units from top row together; do not clip thread. Repeat for next row; then continue for any remaining rows. Remove chainstitched units from machine; do not clip units apart.

2) **Stitch** the next unit of each row to stitched units, starting with top row. Remove chainstitched units from machine; do not clip units apart. Repeat to join any remaining units.

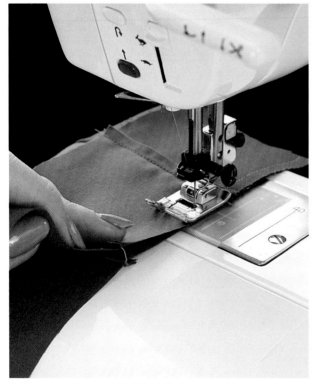

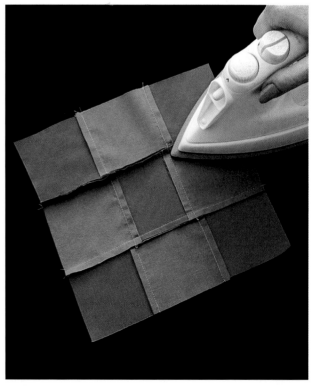

3) **Stitch** the rows together, finger-pressing the seam allowances in opposite directions.

4) **Press** long seam allowances to one side; then press the block from the right side.

Basting a Quilt

Basting is used to hold the quilt top, batting, and backing together while quilting. For ease in handling, the backing and batting should extend 2" to 4" (5 to 10 cm) beyond the edges of the quilt top on all sides.

Before layering and basting, press the quilt top and backing fabric and mark any quilting design lines as on page 119.

Follow the manufacturer's recommendations for pretreating the batting. Some battings require rinsing or washing with soap before using them. If you are using polyester batting, unroll the batting and lay it flat for several hours to allow the wrinkles to smooth out.

Traditionally, quilts were basted using a needle and thread; however, for a faster method, safety-pin basting may be used instead. Lay the quilt flat on a hard surface, such as the floor or a large table, and baste the entire quilt about every 6" (15 cm). If basting with thread, use white cotton thread and a large milliners or darning needle. Use a running stitch about 1" (2.5 cm) long. If basting with safety pins, use rustproof pins.

How to Layer and Baste a Quilt

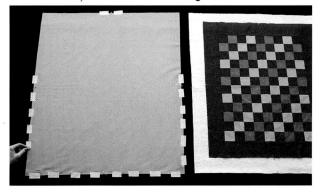

1) Mark center of each side of quilt top at raw edges with safety pins; repeat for batting and backing. Tape the backing, wrong side up, on work surface; begin at the center of each side and work toward the corners, stretching fabric slightly. Backing should be taut, but not stretched.

2) Place batting over backing, matching the pins on each side. Smooth, but do not stretch, working from center of quilt out to sides. Place quilt top right side up over the batting, matching the pins; smooth, but do not stretch.

3) Baste with safety pins or thread, from the center of the quilt to pins on sides; if thread-basting, pull the stitches snug so the layers will not shift, and backstitch at ends. Avoid basting on marked quilting lines or through seams. (Both basting methods are shown.)

4) Baste one quarter-section with safety pins or thread, in parallel rows about 6" (15 cm) apart, working toward the raw edges. If thread-basting, also baste quarter-section in parallel rows in opposite direction. Repeat for remaining quarter-sections.

5) Remove tape from backing. Fold edges of backing over the batting and edges of quilt top to prevent raw edges of fabric from raveling and to prevent the batting from catching on needle and feed dogs during quilting. Pin-baste.

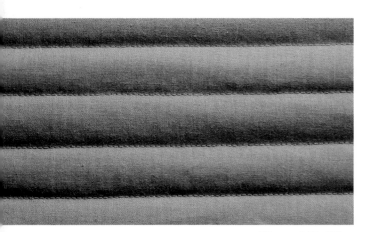

Stitch-in-the-ditch Quilting

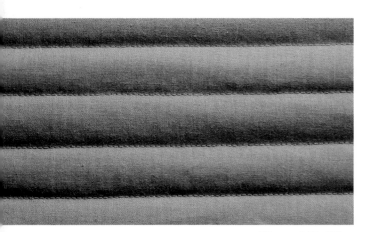

Channel Quilting

Free-motion Motif Quilting

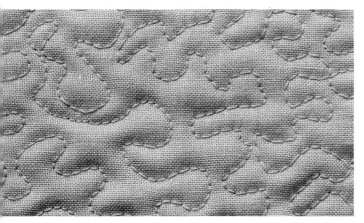

Stipple Quilting

Quilting Basics

Machine quilting is used to hold the layers of the quilt together, but it also adds surface texture and depth to the quilt. A large variety of quilting designs can be created using either machine-guided or free-motion quilting or a combination of both. Plan quilting designs to cover the quilt uniformly, because heavily quilted areas tend to shrink the fabric more than lightly quilted areas.

Machine-guided Quilting

In machine-guided quilting, the feed dogs and the presser foot guide the fabric. This method of quilting is used for stitching long, straight lines or slight curves, and includes stitch-in-the-ditch quilting and channel quilting.

Stitch-in-the-ditch quilting is used to give definition to the blocks, borders, and sashing. It is the easiest method of quilting, and is often the only type of quilting needed to complete a project.

Channel quilting is the stitching of parallel lines. The quilting lines may be either diagonal, vertical, or horizontal and are usually evenly spaced. Mark the quilting lines with a straightedge.

Free-motion Quilting

In free-motion quilting, the quilt top is guided by hand, allowing you to stitch in any direction without repositioning the quilt. The feed dogs are covered or dropped for this method of quilting. Free-motion quilting is used to quilt designs with sharp turns and intricate curves, and includes template quilting, motif quilting, and stipple quilting.

Motif quilting is used to emphasize the printed design of a fabric and is accomplished by outlining the desired motifs. Continue stitching from one motif to the next without stopping. Although free-motion is frequently used for this type of quilting, machine-guided quilting can be used if the motifs consist of subtle curves or if the quilted project is small and can be manipulated easily under the presser foot.

Stipple quilting is used to fill in the background. It can be used to create areas of textured fabric. For uniformity throughout a project, it is best to use loose stipple quilting when combining this method with other types of quilting.

Marking the Quilting Design

With some methods of quilting, it is necessary to mark the quilt before you begin. For channel quilting, mark the design on the quilt top before layering and basting, using a pencil or marking pencil intended for quilting. For stitch-in-the-ditch quilting, motif quilting, and stipple quilting, it is not necessary to mark the quilt top.

If marking designs with pencils, test the pencils on a fabric scrap before using them on the quilt to be sure that the markings do not rub off too easily, but that they can be thoroughly brushed or erased away with a fabric eraser after quilting. Avoid using water-soluble marking pens, because the entire quilt must be rinsed thoroughly to completely remove the markings.

Press quilt top; place on hard surface, with corners squared and sides parallel. Tape securely, keeping quilt top smooth and taut. Mark the quilting design, using straightedge as a guide, beginning at corners of quilt. Mark thin lines, using light pressure.

Stitching & Handling

Cotton thread is traditionally used for quilting. Select the thread color according to how much you want the stitching to show. To avoid changing thread colors often, select one thread color that blends with all the fabrics in the quilt top. Or, to emphasize the quilting stitches and to add embellishment, select a contrasting thread for the quilting, choosing from a variety of different threads, including cotton, polyester, rayon, metallic, and hologram. When quilting with metallic thread, use a needle designed for stitching with metallic thread to prevent shredding and to eliminate skipped stitches. Heavier decorative thread may require a size 16 or 18 needle. When using decorative threads for quilting, thread the machine, and loosen the needle thread tension, if necessary, so the bobbin thread does not show on the right side.

To maintain an even stitch length and to help the quilt feed through the machine evenly, do not allow the quilt to hang over the back or side of the sewing table. Set up the sewing area so the quilt will be supported both to the left of and behind the sewing machine.

Small projects are easily maneuvered as you machine-quilt. Before quilting larger projects, roll up one side of the quilt to allow it to fit on the sewing machine bed. If the sewing surface is not large enough to hold the remaining width, roll up both sides of the quilt.

Plan the sequence of the quilting before you begin to stitch. Begin by anchoring the quilt horizontally and vertically by stitching in the ditch of a seamline near the center and then stitching along any borders; this prevents the layers from shifting. Next, stitch along any sashing strips or between blocks. Once the quilt has been anchored into sections, quilt the areas within the blocks and borders.

Stitch continuously, with as few starts and stops as possible. Prevent tucks from being stitched in the backing fabric by feeling through the layers of the quilt ahead of the sewing machine needle and continuously easing in any excess fabric before it reaches the needle. If a tuck does occur, release the stitches for 3" (7.5 cm) or more and restitch, easing in excess fabric.

Quilting Techniques

For machine-guided quilting, such as stitch-in-the-ditch and channel quilting, it is helpful to stitch with an Even Feed® foot, or walking foot, if one is available; this type of presser foot helps to prevent puckering. Position your hands on either side of the presser foot and hold the fabric taut to prevent the layers from shifting. Stitch, using a stitch length of 10 to 12 stitches per inch (2.5 cm), and ease any excess fabric under the foot as you stitch. The presser foot and feed dogs guide the quilt through the machine.

For free-motion quilting, such as template, motif, and stipple quilting, remove the regular presser foot and attach a darning foot. Set the machine for a straight stitch, and use a straight-stitch needle plate; cover the feed dogs, or lower them. It is not necessary to adjust the stitch length setting on the machine, because the stitch length is determined by a combination of the movement of the quilt and the speed of the needle. Use your hands to guide the fabric as you stitch, applying gentle tension. With the presser foot lifter in the lowered position, stitch, moving the fabric with wrist and hand movements. Maintain a steady rhythm and speed as you stitch, to keep the stitch length uniform. When changing your hand positions, stop stitching, with the needle down in the fabric.

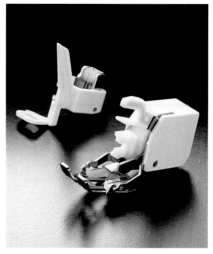

Presser feet recommended for quilting include the darning foot (left) and the Even Feed or walking foot (right). An Even Feed foot is used for machine-guided quilting. A darning foot is used for free-motion quilting.

How to Quilt Using Machine-guided Techniques

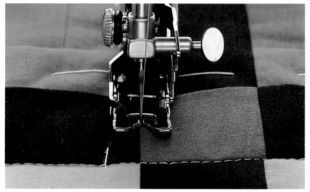

Stitch-in-the-ditch quilting. Stitch over the seamline, stitching in the well of the seam.

Channel quilting. Stitch parallel quilting lines, starting with inner marked line and working outward.

How to Quilt Using Free-motion Techniques

Free-motion motif quilting. Determine the longest continuous stitching line possible; stitch. Stitch additional design lines as necessary.

Stipple quilting. Stitch random, curving lines. Work in small sections, keeping spaces between quilting lines close; do not cross over lines. Work from edges toward center, covering background uniformly.

Binding a Quilt

Double binding provides durable finished edges for quilts. The binding can be cut to match the border of the quilt, or it can be cut from a fabric that coordinates with the pieced quilt top.

Double binding, cut on the straight of grain, has two popular finished widths. Regular binding has a finished width of a scant ½" (1.3 cm), and narrow binding has a finished width of a scant ⅜" (1 cm). Regular binding is used for most quilts; cut the binding strips 2½" (6.5 cm) wide. Narrow binding is used for small quilts, such as wall hangings that are 36" (91.5 cm) or smaller; cut the binding strips 2" (5 cm) wide.

The directions for each quilt in this book specify either regular or narrow binding, and the required binding yardage is given. Binding strips are cut on the crosswise grain of the fabric and pieced to the necessary length.

How to Bind a Quilt with Double Binding

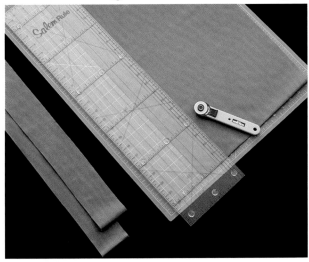

1) Fold the fabric in half on the lengthwise grain. On the crosswise grain, cut strips 2½" (6.5 cm) wide for regular binding or 2" (5 cm) wide for narrow binding.

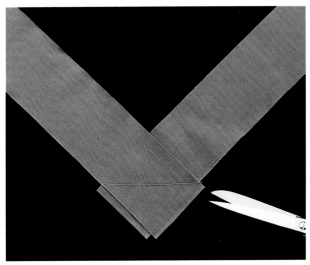

2) Pin strips, right sides together, at right angles, if it is necessary to piece binding strips; strips will form a V. Stitch diagonally across strips.

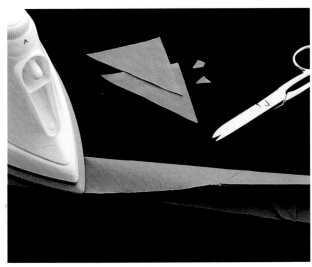

3) Trim seam allowances to ¼" (6 mm). Press seam open. Trim points even with edges. Press the binding strip in half lengthwise, wrong sides together.

4) Measure quilt top across middle. Cut two binding strips equal to this measurement plus 2" (5 cm). Mark binding strips 1" (2.5 cm) from ends; divide area between pins in fourths, and pin-mark. Divide upper and lower edges of quilt in fourths; pin-mark.

(Continued on next page)

5) Place the binding strip on upper edge of quilt top, matching the raw edges and pin marks; binding will extend 1" (2.5 cm) beyond quilt top at each end. Pin binding along length, easing in any fullness.

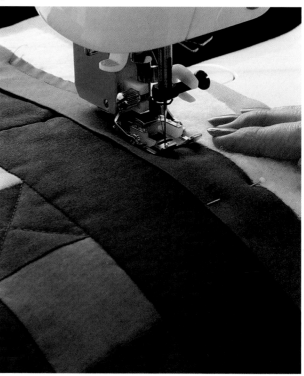

6) Stitch binding strip to the quilt, a scant ¼" (6 mm) from raw edges of binding.

7) Trim the excess batting and backing to a scant ½" (1.3 cm) from stitching for regular binding; trim to a scant ⅜" (1 cm) for narrow binding.

8) Wrap binding strip snugly around edge of quilt, covering stitching line on back of quilt; pin in the ditch of the seam.

9) **Stitch in the ditch** on right side of quilt, catching binding on back of quilt.

10) **Repeat** steps 5 to 9 for lower edge of quilt. Trim ends of upper and lower binding strips even with the edges of quilt top.

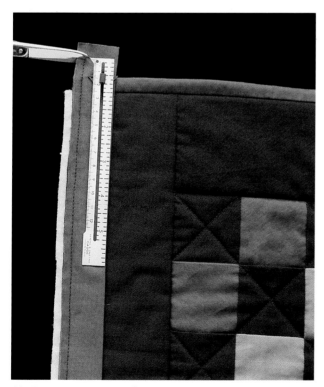

11) **Repeat** steps 4 to 7 for sides of quilt, measuring the quilt top down middle in step 4. Trim the ends of binding strips to extend ½" (1.3 cm) beyond the finished edges of quilt.

12) **Fold** binding along the stitching line. Fold ½" (1.3 cm) ends of binding over finished edges; glue, using glue stick. Wrap binding around edges; glue in place, and stitch in the ditch as in steps 8 and 9.

Hanging a Quilt

For a quilt to be displayed as a wall hanging, the weight of the quilt must be distributed evenly. Attach a fabric sleeve made from unbleached muslin or quilt fabric to the back of the quilt and insert a wooden lath that has been sealed with varnish, polyurethane, or paint. Choose to attach the fabric sleeve into the binding of the quilt or attach it by hand to the back of the quilt after the quilt is finished. To prevent fading or fabric deterioration, display quilts away from direct sunlight or bright, constant artificial light and vacuum them occasionally.

How to Make and Attach a Fabric Sleeve to a Finished Quilt

1) Cut a piece of fabric or muslin 10" (25.5 cm) wide by the width of the quilt. Turn under and stitch ½" (1.3 cm) double-fold hems at short ends. Stitch the long edges of the strip, right sides together, in ½" (1.3 cm) seam; press seam allowances open. Turn sleeve right side out; press flat, centering seam.

2) Pin the sleeve to the back of the quilt, close to edges. Hand-stitch the sleeve to quilt along upper and lower edges; stitch through backing and into batting.

3) Cut a wooden lath ½" (1.3 cm) shorter than width of quilt; insert lath through sleeve. Secure lath to wall, placing screws or nails at ends of lath.

How to Make and Attach a Fabric Sleeve into the Binding of the Quilt

1) Cut a piece of fabric or muslin 6" (15 cm) wide by the width of the quilt. Turn under and stitch ½" (1.3 cm) double-fold hems at short ends. Fold in half lengthwise, matching raw edges; press.

2) Follow pages 121 to 122, steps 1 to 7, for binding. Center and pin fabric sleeve to upper edge of quilt on the back side, lapping long raw edges of sleeve ¼" (6 mm) over stitching line of binding. Machine-baste the fabric sleeve to quilt by stitching just inside the previous stitching on binding side of quilt.

3) Continue to apply binding as on pages 122 to 123, steps 8 to 12. Pin lower edge of sleeve to quilt; hand-stitch in place, stitching through backing and into batting. Hang quilt as in step 3, above.

Embellishing Ideas

Create quilts that are visually exciting by incorporating a variety of embellishment techniques. Using decorative thread for quilting adds subtle interest to the quilt. Other soft embellishments may include appliquéd designs, fabric yo-yos, lace, and ribbon. You can even layer sheer fabrics, such as organza or tulle, over your quilt blocks to create interesting effects. For dimensional interest, apply embellishments such as buttons, beads, charms, or tassels. Or use silk ribbon embroidery to give highlights to your quilt.

Decorative threads, from top to bottom, include: metallic, rayon, hologram, and variegated.

Dimensional embellishments include decorative beads, buttons, charms, tassels, and silk ribbon embroidery.

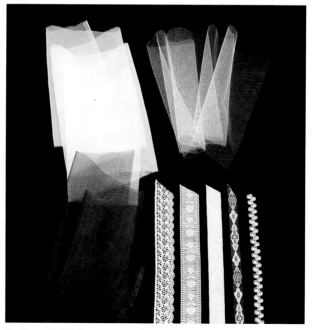

Appliqués such as fabric yo-yos, raw-edge appliqués, and thread lace give additional interest and texture to quilt projects.

Soft embellishments such as organza, glitter organza, tulle, net, ribbon, and lace add variety to the surface of a quilt.

Index

Cowles Creative Publishing, Inc. offers a variety of how-to books. For information write:

   Cowles Creative Publishing, Inc.
   Subscriber Books
   5900 Green Oak Drive
   Minnetonka, MN 55343